Balanced Teshuvah

MOSAICA PRESS

JENNY SERLE

Balanced
Teshuvah

*Guidance and Inspiration
for Baalei Teshuvah*

Mosaica Press, Inc.
© 2019 by Mosaica Press
Designed and typeset by Brocha Mirel Strizower

ISBN-10: 1-946351-52-0
ISBN-13: 978-1-946351-52-4

Published by:
Mosaica Press, Inc.
www.mosaicapress.com
info@mosaicapress.com

This book is dedicated to my parents,

Michael and Ella Stesel

*Thank you for instilling within us the abilities to explore
and then navigate a Torah life. May you see all the
fruits of your labor and enjoy the nachas you deserve
from your children and grandchildren. Hashem should
grant you health and strength to continue investing
yourselves, in every way, in every single one of us—
from smallest to biggest, until 120.*

יחיאל מיכל טווערסקי

כאאפויר חרה"צ כמזהר"ר יעקב ישראל זצללה"ה מהארלאסטייפאל

Rabbi Michel Twerski

29 Iyar 5778

To Bnai Yisroel Everywhere י"צו:

I was deeply impressed as I paged through Jenny Serle's manuscript, <u>Balanced Teshuva</u>, to find a very lucid, practical, and on-target exposition of the challenging world of the Ba'al Teshuvah.   Serle's book touches on virtually every relevant aspect of the Ba'al Teshuvah's journey, offering cogent, practical, and common sense insights into how the newcomer can integrate and manage a complex, new world. This book should be mandatory reading, not only for the stranger to the Torah world, but to every frume family that is part of welcoming these courageous neshomois and supporting them in their growth. Knowing and understanding the problems, past, present and future, facing these intrepid travelers, will enable both professional Mekarvim and lay members of the community to offer empathic, useful counsel, paving the way for the Ba'alei Teshuvah's optimal progress. I highly recommend this very important work, and offer my personal blessings that it be well received in Jewish communities everywhere.

With warmest brachois for hatzlacha,

Rabbi Michel Twerski

מוסדות אור שמח מרכז טננבאום ע.ר. 58-00-21343-00
רח׳ שמעון הצדיק 22-28 ירושלים ת.ד. 18103
טל: 02-581-0315

Tammuz 5778

Baruch Hashem, recent decades have seen the return of thousands of Jews to their eternal heritage. While there is still much to be done, the *baal teshuvah* movement is eloquent testimony to the indestructible holiness of the Jewish soul, the *pintele yid*, the light that cannot be extinguished despite decades of assimilation. The men and women who have had the courage to dramatically change their lives inspire all of us with their passion, depth and spirituality; the relationship between the BT (newly-observant) and the FFB (*frum* from birth) is a reciprocal one — each elevating and inspiring the other, each helping the other grow but in turn growing as well in the process.

But the transition to becoming a full-fledged member of the religious community can be fraught with difficulty. The *baal teshuvah* may lack the family connections, the familiarity with *frum* "culture," the experience of seeing religious life acted out in the day-to-day mundane activities of marriage and parenting. As the euphoria of the yeshiva and seminary with its constant emphasis on spirituality and growth yields to the everyday demands of making a living and running a home, the *baal teshuvah* may experience a disillusionment as he/she realizes that in some ways, they face the same problems as everyone else, and the Torah was not a magic elixir. Many who work in Jewish outreach have understood for a long time that side by side with all the wonderful books and classes that bring people to Judaism, we need concrete practical guidance for the people who have already made the commitment. It is not enough to abandon them to their own devices and simply focus on bringing in new recruits.

Fortunately, Jenny Serle has given us the book that addresses these issues. In eleven well-organized chapters, she ably addresses the difficulties of bridging worlds, the importance of having a *rav*, dating, marriage, parenting, choosing a community, keeping inspiration, dealing with the occasional disappointment one might have in the religious community or particular members of it, striving for greatness, and a host of other issues. The book is filled with practical advice based on real-world life experience. To her great credit, the author is honest and open in spelling out the difficulties the *baal teshuvah* will face in adjusting to his/her new world; she does not attempt to cover up problems when they exist. But she never allows her clear-eyed critiques to turn into cynicism and negativity. She reminds the reader of the true beauty of a Torah life and the beauty of finding one's place within a community of people who strive to live up to its values. She reminds the *baal teshuvah* of the reasons they became observant and how those reasons are still valid. The *frum* world is not perfect because human beings are not perfect, but the tone of this work is profoundly optimistic and uplifting. The author's message is: Keep your eyes open, know the facts, be ready for some tough times and turbulent waters, but know that it is all worth it. Her genuine love for Hashem, Torah and Am Yisrael is apparent on every page.

My hope and prayer is that this wonderful work reach its intended audience, that it will inform, inspire and uplift both the *chozrei b'teshuvah* and the broader Jewish community; and that it will increase love among Jews and add to the glory of the Creator.

With much *brachah*,

Yitzchak A. Breitowitz
Rav, Kehillas Ohr Somayach, Jerusalem

בס"ד

ז' אב תשע"ח

It was with great pleasure that I received and read the manuscript for *Balanced Teshuvah* by Mrs. Jenny Serle. As someone who has had the privilege of working with many *baalei teshuvah* over the years, I have long felt that there is a need for a work that would help those who have committed themselves to a life of Torah and *mitzvos* deal with the challenge of how to actually live that life, as frum Jews and as part of the frum community, in a healthy and balanced way. *Balanced Teshuvah* meets this need. The author has helped many singles and young families who are new to *Yiddishkeit* adjust to their new reality, through her individual guidance and public lectures. In her book, she answers many questions for those going through the adjustment process. *How do I deal with my non-frum parents and family? How do I know which minhagim to take on? What role should my mentor play in my life? How do I find a rav for myself and my family?* These, and many other issues, are dealt with in *Balanced Teshuvah* with clarity and sensitivity. I am confident that it will be of great help both to *baalei teshuvah* and their mentors.

This book was a particular *nachas* for me, as I have known the author since she was my student in high school. I wish her much continued success in helping לקרב לבבות לאבינו שבשמים.

בברכה,
Rabbi Reuven Gross

Table of Contents

Acknowledgments

The Jewish people are often referred to as "*Yehudim*," after Yaakov Avinu's son, one of the twelve *Shevatim*, Yehuda. At its essence, the name Yehuda carries with it the notion of "*hodaah*," gratitude. At the core of the Jewish mentality is the experience of gratitude. To be grateful is to acknowledge the contributions of those around you. It is to recognize that without these, you would be severely lacking in ability to produce or accomplish that which you strive for. Words are inadequate to express the overwhelming gratitude I feel, and which is rightfully due to those who have helped me.

The greatest *hakaras ha'tov* in this world is due to the Master of the Universe. To see God's Hand in orchestrating the details of my life and in guiding me toward the places where He allows me to shine His light arouses the deepest feeling of awe and gratitude. I am indebted by the great *berachos* He continually gives me, and I feel the urgency to utilize these for the greatest possible contribution to His people and world.

To Rabbis Haber and Kornbluth, and the entire talented staff at Mosaica Press, I would like to express my appreciation for helping me improve and refine my manuscript into the final product. Your edits and feedback were most insightful and helped me communicate crucial ideas more effectively.

To the countless young women who have trusted me with their triumphs, their struggles, their stories, and journeys. You have given me insight into the greatness of Hashem's people. I've grown immensely through connecting to you, and your dedication and strength have inspired me to greater levels of *ahavas Yisrael*. Your true potential to shine already exists deep within; I am humbled that you have invited me to help you discover and access it.

To Rabbi Reuven Gross, *rav* of Congregation Shaarei Tzedek in Chicago, for the countless hours you have invested in teaching and guiding me—going all the way back to high school, where your insights helped shape my perspectives and personal trajectory, and in more recent years, for providing personal guidance to our family as well as helping to navigate our way in guiding others. The insights and wisdom that you imparted for this work in particular, when you reviewed the topics in their original class format, have greatly impacted the ideas presented here. Your ability to integrate *daas Torah* with the nuances that apply to individuals and specific situations is incredible and has proven invaluable to our family. It is something we try to emulate as we give over to others as well.

To my closest friends, confidants, greatest role models, and first Torah teachers. It is rare for any person to embody so many things, and yet my brother and sister-in-law (who is really a sister to me in her own right), Max and Irina Stesel, do just that. The sincerity and depth of your *ahavas Yisrael* is unparalleled. Your dedication to the Jewish people is not only inspiring but has truly formed the basis of my own goals and dreams. Our special relationship is among the greatest *berachos* in my life.

To my in-laws, Brian Serle and Lynn Harris, for all of your warmth and love. Your encouragement is always appreciated. Most of all, thank you for the greatest gift you could give the children and I—our wonderful husband and father.

To my parents, Michael and Ella Stesel, to whom this book is dedicated. You have selflessly given me everything I have ever needed to grow, develop, and pursue my goals and dreams. You have relentlessly believed in my abilities and supported me in every endeavor. You instilled Torah values in our family and home, long before we formally learned of these. Your sense of dignity, regalness, true *simchah*, dedication, and commitment to our family and to truth made our exploration of and connection to Torah Judaism a most natural one. Your love and wisdom guide us and give us the wherewithal to continue to grow and to build.

To our children, Yaakov, Aviva, Aryeh, and Shani. You continually expand me and Tatty in immeasurable ways. Seeing each of you, with your very unique and special personalities, strengths, and potentials is an incredible journey into experiencing Hashem's beautiful world in a multifaceted and exciting way. Each of you should continue to grow *mi'chayil el chayil* and always know how much Hashem, Tatty, and I love you and believe in you. We can't wait to see you shine your unique lights brighter and brighter and light up Hashem's world with all that each of you has to offer.

To my husband, Yonason, for being my greatest source of support and inspiration. Your wisdom and deep strength are the bedrock of our family and everything I do. It is impossible to truly thank you for your uncommon degree of dedication to everything that is important to you. Having you by my side as a true partner through the journey of life makes the possibilities feel limitless and the experience infinitely richer.

Introduction

O nly a few generations ago, the phenomenon of secular Jews adopting an observant lifestyle was nearly unheard of. When Jews began to return, it was seen as nothing short of a miracle. And here we are today, with hundreds of thousands of Jews who have become more observant. The modern Baal Teshuvah movement is not only a testimony to the power of Torah but also to the strength of an individual, to the *pintele Yid*—that part of Avraham Avinu in each of us.

And yet, our journey is far from over. Because now we have to walk this path and navigate it successfully in a way that we were not prepared for explicitly from birth and upbringing. Just like we were critical thinking, deep searching, and proactive in getting here, so too must we use these same qualities in furthering ourselves. By clearly perceiving our unique potential as contributive, well-integrated members of the Jewish community, we foster the success not only of our own journey but that of our children as well.

As *baalei teshuvah* exit the safe cocoon of their initial exposure to the warmth and beauty of Judaism, they find themselves in a foreign culture, often not knowing the language and dynamics of their observant community, and facing unexpected situations they may feel unprepared for. Moreover, they often find themselves alone in dealing with these new challenges. This scenario can result in feelings of inadequacy, insecurity, and even in questioning their decision to go through the hardships of changing their entire lifestyle in the first place.

This is not only the experience of someone who became observant a short time ago. This can be, and often is, the reality of men and women, of mothers and fathers, who have been living observant lives for many years. Even as time progresses and they become settled in their lives, a feeling of insecurity sometimes prevails.

It may feel daunting to enter a *frum* community and become an active member there, to walk into a new shul, to try out different shuls for the "right fit," or to choose a school for our kids and then feel capable of navigating the inevitable politics there. On the one hand, we don't want to feel like we always stand out in dress, speech, or other ways. On the other hand, we also don't want to lose our individuality or our identity, which were the keys to our growth and success until this point.

What is the solution? How can *baalei teshuvah* manage?

As in most areas in life, an innate sense of competency is a great indicator of success in the endeavor at hand. The overarching aim of this book is to provide the tools necessary to develop confidence within each *baal teshuvah*, building an awareness of their ability to successfully integrate into the *frum* community and lead productive, healthy lives there.

Rabbi Avraham Twerski[1] offers an incredible insight. He says that the words "*baal teshuvah*" mean the "owner of the answer." The obvious question is: Which question is he answering? Rabbi Twerski says that the *baal teshuvah* answers the *original* question. In *Bereishis*, Hashem says to Adam, "*Ayeka*—Where are you?" We know that Hashem is not in need of a tracking device! He is not asking for Adam's physical location. Rather, He is saying, "What have you done with your life; what do you intend to do with it?" Adam got the answer wrong. He said, "I heard your voice and I feared you because I am naked, so I hid." In essence, Adam hid because he couldn't face himself, so he certainly couldn't face Hashem in his shameful state of having committed wrongdoing. In contrast, each and every *baal teshuvah* has answered the question correctly, accurately perceiving this not as a one-time question but rather as a

---

1   Lisa Aiken, PhD, *The Baal Teshuva Survival Guide* (Rossi Publications, 2009), Foreword.

perpetual question that challenges humanity as a whole, as well as each individual, throughout all of history.

We have recognized the truth of our *neshamah*, the Divine part within us, and this recognition has allowed us to leave the state of feeling naked. Our years of hard work in deepening our awareness of where we are heading and where we stand now have allowed us to define and determine our trajectory. We have no reason to hide from Hashem—or from ourselves. We can, and should, feel free and empowered by the knowledge we have acquired, harnessing it as a guiding light to build our lives and express our *neshamahs*, as we leave the unique imprint of our talents and abilities upon our families and our communities.

In his introduction to *Mesilas Yesharim*, the Ramchal (Rabbi Moshe Chaim Luzzatto) states that even things that are known and perhaps obvious are important to think through and review. In that spirit, much of what is presented in this book is not new information. Rather, we are presenting commonly known information, from a reframed and focused perspective. It is crucial to delve into these topics, think through the ideas presented, and process them, as they are often severely under-addressed in our communities and in the midst of our hectic lives.

In many ways, this book is the result of witnessing and having had the *zechus* to be an intimate part of the journey to Torah Judaism and then the journey within it, with countless individuals, for over a decade. It is the result of the awe I have experienced in seeing individuals confront themselves and their lives with incredible honesty and then continuing on to transform themselves according to the values and truths they discovered, with unparalleled strength and dedication. It is also the result of seeing the frustration men and women feel when they fail to feel successful in the very thing they fought so hard for.

Having gone through the process of discovering and taking on Torah observance firsthand, and subsequently working in outreach—first with adolescents and then with young professionals—for over a decade, I began to identify trends in the challenges and experiences of those individuals who went on to embrace a Torah-observant lifestyle. I also noticed that within our communities there is a large investment of resources—time, energy, and finances—allocated to both community institutions (e.g., schools and shuls) and organized outreach efforts. Both of these are necessary and invaluable causes that deserve our attention and input.

Yet there is one group in the middle, having moved beyond the initial *kiruv* experiences but not quite feeling comfortable or confident in their established *frum* environment, which is not being addressed adequately. The *baal teshuvah* population has unique needs, questions, challenges, and experiences—all of which need to be validated and explored. Tailored guidance and support need to be given to individuals at this next phase in their Jewish journey, thereby enabling *baalei teshuvah* to deepen their roots in Torah communities.

Several years ago, when I first announced a series of classes focusing on topics specific to *baalei teshuvah*, the response was overwhelming and confirmed these feelings. It was obvious that people, regardless of how many years they have been *frum*, felt a real need to discuss and process the *baal teshuvah* experience in this way. Since that first class, I have taught this series many times over the ensuing years, both to local cohorts in the Chicago area and nationally via webinar. With each series, the material was expanded, refined, and reviewed until it eventually formed the basis of this book. The ideas and perspectives presented have been developed over many years, both through my own personal experiences as well as through teaching and guiding *baalei teshuvah*, who began their journeys in many different ways, yet share many experiences in common at this next stage. This book was created to reinforce, guide, and, most of all, serve as a reminder of the inherent capability each person possesses to live fulfilled, successful lives as Torah Jews.

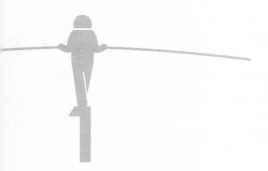

Bridging Worlds:
Dealing with Our Secular Past, Family, and Friends

Understanding Our Past

Ramchal[2] discusses the idea that every person is given a piece of Hashem's "unity," which he or she is supposed to reveal throughout their lifetime. Just as the facets of a diamond, where each surface, with its unique angle, shape, and depth, needs the other in order to reveal the breathtaking sparkle within, so too each person is given their individual set of tools—their background, personality, strengths, and challenges—which they can channel as a conduit for Hashem's light to shine outward. In so doing, they can accomplish something unique and Godly, becoming a *kiddush Hashem* in this world. Negating these factors denies their purpose, causing a type of

---

2   *Daas Tevunos* 40.

atrophy to the very muscles one is meant to use in making a unique contribution to Hashem's world.

Hashem did not make a mistake raising a Jew to be nonobservant. It is not *b'dieved*. It is the very task Hashem designated for them. Just as Hashem could have easily sent the *baal teshuvah* to be born and raised in an observant family, His decision not to do so must have been for good reason. Acknowledging this fact is the key to enabling the *baal teshuvah* to channel his or her past experiences to glorify the Torah in a way that only they are capable of.

The Talmud describes how Reish Lakish's remarkable strength, which had enabled him to succeed as a thief, could be redirected to enable him to become a great Torah scholar.[3] So unique was he that after his death, his *chavrusa* and brother-in-law, Rabbi Yochanan, wasn't able to find a satisfactory study partner. There were many Torah scholars in Eretz Yisrael at that time, yet we are told that only Reish Lakish could challenge Rabbi Yochanan in the sharpest way, using his powerful nature and strength to express deep questions and arguments. In this way, it was because of—not in spite of—his past and identity that he was able to later become a Torah giant.

Baalei teshuvah often feel bad about mistakes they have made in the past, feeling somehow tainted as a result of their experiences in the secular world. *Rambam* outlines[4] the process of *teshuvah* as follows: The individual must

1. feel regret for their wrongdoing;
2. distance themselves from their mistake;
3. verbalize their error;
4. resolve to change their behavior moving forward.

Guilt and regret are only positive and necessary forces insofar as they are a conduit for change and self-improvement. Lingering guilt is unnecessary and is a negative force, preventing true change and forward movement. We are taught that real *teshuvah* not only erases our errors

---

3   *Bava Metzia* 84a.
4   *Hilchos Teshuvah* 2:2.

but turns the very *aveiros* into mitzvos that stand as shining badges of honor on our *neshamos*.[5]

Teshuvah, in the big picture, is the process of wanting and then striving to do better, to be a more authentic version of oneself who can then develop a deep and close personal relationship with Hashem. Any voice that says to someone, "Look at the awful *aveiros* you've done. They're so bad that you're beyond repair," is the voice of the *yetzer hara*. It may sound scholarly and even holy, but it is the *yetzer hara* in sophisticated disguise. If it were Hashem's voice, it may say something along the lines of, "I know you've made mistakes and I know you've had struggles. I set you up for those. I gave you those challenges. I understand why you were challenged by them. I see you trying to do better, to be your best. I know you can do it. And I want you to know that the person you'll meet on the other side of this challenge is more refined, more developed, stronger, and deeper than another who never went through it in the first place."

Indeed, as Hashem helped us through the challenges we faced, He no doubt saw this greater, more elevated version of ourselves slowly being formed. We should see it in ourselves and appreciate the great, unique *kiddush Hashem* we bring to the world through—and not despite—these experiences.

Rav Dessler, *zt"l*, asks the reader to imagine a ceremony celebrating the king who rules in a certain land. His subjects all prepare speeches in his honor. The first one gets up and begins expounding on the virtues and greatness of the king. A second subject stands and repeats the speech of the first one verbatim. A third gets up and says the exact same thing. And so on and so forth, until hundreds of people in the kingdom have repeated the same words of praise to the king.

Rav Dessler asks: Is this honorable to the king? Does it truly praise him? Or, instead, is it a disgrace, an insult to the greatness of the king, that only one thing has been said even though he has countless subjects in his kingdom?[6]

---

5   *Yoma* 86b.
6   Rabbi Eliyahu E. Dessler in A. Carmell (ed.), *Strive for Truth* (Jerusalem: Feldheim, 1978), p. 89; *Michtav Me'Eliyahu* (Jerusalem: Sifriati, 2002), p. 22.

So too, Hashem created a myriad of people and situations, each with their unique family and personal dynamics, details, and traits. None of these are to our disadvantage. Hashem is waiting for us to utilize the very same abilities that we employed along the journey to observance as a means to create *kiddush Hashem* in the world while we continue down this path.

How We Got Here

An important part of this discussion is to remember that no one "made us *frum*." We were not passive. While we had mentors, teachers, and support along the way, we are the ones who integrated information that was presented to us and put in great effort and energy to overcome all the various challenges that are inherent to changing one's lifestyle. There were resources and people that facilitated our climb. Nonetheless, it was we who climbed. They cheered us on, taught us the skill of climbing, and gave us exercises to strengthen our muscles as we prepared to ascend. Still, the climb is ours, and reaching the destination is to our credit as well. To this end, there is no individual and no organization that owns us or our accomplishments (or failures!). It is important to feel *hakaras ha'tov*, a sincere sense of gratitude, to the people along the way for being there to assist us. Our recognition and gratitude for the support and numerous contributions of all those who helped us along our journey is appropriate and correct. In contrast, our decision to continue a particular relationship with a previous guide or mentor, or to align ourselves with a specific segment of the Orthodox community, should remain within our realm of individual choice, unhindered by feelings of indebtedness to others.

Baalei teshuvah often find themselves vulnerable when they feel pressure to continue seeking guidance from a particular person or to identify with the same *hashkafic* outlook as the individuals who had the *zechus* to be a part of their Jewish journey. This is neither appropriate nor healthy. A strongly rooted Torah life comes as a result of taking personal responsibility for life decisions—within the framework of halachah—that resonate deeply within because they reflect one's unique identity. Without this awareness, a person may end up living a life that isn't truly their own, experiencing greater internal discord as time goes on, as a person can only role-play for so long.

> *A recently frum yeshiva bachur once arrived for a Shabbos meal with a married avreich. The avreich, now in his late forties, had taken on mitzvah observance in his early twenties. During a quiet moment at the meal, the avreich turned to the young guest and said, "You know, sometimes I look in the mirror and don't even recognize the person I see in the reflection."*

We should become more than we are in the present moment, but that growth should be our own. We have to be able to see ourselves in the process as we engage in it, and even more, we should strive to see the highest version of ourselves. We must recognize the life and the person we are creating and building with every decision made along the way.

> *I once had a student who switched from public school to a Jewish day school. One of the people who helped make this transition possible made sure to utilize most encounters with her to remind her that "she owes it to the people who got her here" to maintain a certain religious standing and profile and adhere to the standards of the community that she was now affiliated with.*

While the mentor or teacher certainly means well, and the messages communicated are typically not nearly as overt or intentional as the one in the above anecdote, pressure is often felt by the *baal teshuvah*, upon whom it takes its toll. If, out of frustration, he or she eventually becomes motivated to extricate themselves from this pressure, they will again begin to look for the true, authentic sense of identity they lost touch with long ago. Quite possibly, they will struggle to find it in religious life because it was never created there in the first place.

> *A young woman had recently come back to her hometown from seminary, having accepted upon herself mitzvah observance. As she settled into the frum community in her city, she realized that, over time, she would need to make a conscious decision to*

identify herself with a particular hashkafah within the spectrum of Orthodox Judaism. In discussing this next phase of her Jewish growth with her rabbi and rebbetzin, she nervously asked, "What if, as I explore the various paths within Torah Judaism, I ultimately end up choosing something that is different from you or your family? Maybe I won't send my kids to the same schools? Or maybe I'll decide that I'd like to implement sensitivities into my future home that are different from yours?"

Her rabbi made sure to assuage her concerns. "We are going to be proud of you no matter which hashkafah ends up resonating most with you. It doesn't have to be exactly the same as ours. You've come so far, and the most important thing is that you continue to grow and build an authentic relationship with Hashem."

This young woman left this conversation greatly relieved and encouraged. She felt free to focus on discovering herself more deeply, striving to perceive the nuanced aspects of *hashkafah* that would most strongly enable her to live a Torah lifestyle filled with joy and sustained growth.

It Takes a Village

When our oldest child turned five, my husband and I decided to visit the different elementary schools in our community in an attempt to determine which would be the best fit for our family and children. At one such visit, I ran into a teacher who had briefly taught at the Hebrew school I attended over a dozen years prior. As we exchanged friendly greetings, he exclaimed with pride, "When I get to Shamayim, I'm going to say your name!" (and presumably the gates would swing open for him).

My first reaction was a desire to warn him that I wasn't so sure my name would be the safest bet in getting him very far over there! In addition, I found the feeling that I was someone's project or trophy to be unsettling. Certainly, every single person along one's journey toward becoming a *baal teshuvah* has tremendous *schar* for their efforts and involvement. In truth, in the life of any one *baal teshuvah*, there are so many people who play vital roles at various stages, no individual gets the "credit" or "owns" parts of this person and their life. The mentality of "I made so-and-so *frum*" is distorted at best and disempowering at worst.

The involvement and contributions of a myriad of individuals for any one *baal teshuvah* is often best illustrated by attending their wedding. Here one is almost guaranteed to find representatives of numerous outreach organizations, spanning cities, continents, and hemispheres. This is natural and it is positive. Many people and institutions played important roles in this person's life that shaped their decisions and eventual steps toward Torah observance. But the sum total of that life is only theirs. Labeling couples as an "organization X" couple or their children as an "organization Y baby" is furthering a false impression of ownership. Instead, *baalei teshuvah* are greatly empowered when they appreciate all those who have helped them along their journey, while also sensing that they are perceived as individuals who have become successful members of their communities on their own merits.

> *A young man who took on observance a number of years ago was learning in yeshiva for several years. At some point, he decided that the next step in his learning and Jewish growth was to switch to another yeshiva, which seemingly offered higher-level class options than what was available at his current institution. As he developed relationships with the rebbeim in his new yeshiva, they frequently encouraged him to seek guidance from the rebbeim in his previous yeshiva as well. They reminded him that his rebbeim there knew him well and were also generally more experienced in advising baalei teshuvah. This experience allowed his transition between schools, as well as within his stages of Jewish growth, to be a positive and healthy one.*

In addition to emphasizing the positive nature of the many sources of input the *baal teshuvah* has had, the individual's sense of self is greatly enhanced when their personal accomplishments are highlighted.

A young woman who became frum a short time ago was spend-
ing Shabbos with the outreach family who had worked on her
college campus while she was a student there. They were her
first Torah teachers and her initial connection to Judaism. She
brought a friend from seminary along with her and introduced
her to the couple, telling her, "I'm so excited for you to meet this
family. This rabbi and rebbetzin made me frum!"

The couple smiled but the rebbetzin responded, "It was so great
to have you participate in our programs and attend our classes,
but remember, there were many, many students who sat
through all the same experiences as you. And yet, the majority
of them, for whatever reason, did not choose to further their
Jewish involvement as you did! We are so glad we could be part
of your journey. But you're the one who made you frum!"

This young woman was deeply touched. She had never thought
about it quite that way. The sentiments of those she respected
built her up in a significant way.

The Ball Is in Your Court

Of course, there is a flip side to this discussion: just like no one "made
us *frum*," it is not anyone else's responsibility to "keep us *frum*" (and
growing). In the following chapters, we will discuss the steps toward
accomplishing this. As a prerequisite, it is important to realize that
continued growth and strengthening of our relationship with Hashem
and Torah is our responsibility.

We are most likely to be successful when we harness our character
traits, talents, and skills, directing them in a productive and purposeful way within our lives as Torah Jews. There are so many areas of the
observant community that will benefit from the unique talents of individuals who didn't grow up "in the system":

- It's not uncommon to hear from parents that the best English
  and math teachers in their children's schools are *baalei teshu-*
  vah. This is a most natural phenomenon. *Baalei teshuvah* often

have advanced language, math, writing, and other skills due to an advanced secular studies background as well as higher levels of education.

- The Jewish music industry is replete with those who come from non-Jewish environments but who have fused Torah ideas with new flavors of rhythm and melody that bring our desire to connect to Hashem and the Jewish people to new levels.
- *Baalei teshuvah* are often at the forefront of outreach. Our fellow brothers and sisters are disappearing at alarming rates due to assimilation. Often, the people who can understand, relate to, and therefore inspire them are the individuals who experienced their struggles and their realities firsthand.
- It is fascinating to see that *baalei teshuvah* are often even on the frontlines of the battle to reengage and inspire disenfranchised Jewish youth and young adults who grew up observant but lacked the positivity, warmth, and excitement that were needed to establish strong roots in their observance.

There are voids waiting to be filled. They are waiting for us to fill them. Only once we've integrated our whole selves into our Torah-observant lives will we be able to address these most important needs.

Taking our innate selves and striving to be the highest version of ourselves is the job and ultimate purpose of every Jew, not just the *baal teshuvah*. Yet if this is the case for everyone, then why does the *baal teshuvah* often resist and feel the need to negate and deny their true selves, instead of redirecting and bringing out the true purpose of these God-given qualities and experiences?

> *I was once approached by the owner of a nursing home company. He told me that one of his facilities was in need of a marketing director and asked if I knew anyone who might be a good fit for the job. I told him I'd think about it and that I might have a few good candidates. After all, I work with an outreach organization that has many active and successful young professionals; certainly someone in the group would be a good fit.*

> *He looked hesitant. "I don't know," he said. "Marketing re-*
> *quires some chutzpah. And, you know, baalei teshuvah have no*
> *chutzpah."*

Most striking to me at the time was the truth in his words. And yet, I thought, how could this be?! How much "chutzpah" did one muster to challenge all the societal norms they were brought up to accept and follow! How much "chutzpah" did it take to confront friends, family, and acquaintances! And to relentlessly commit to one's values and standards of behavior when these were perceived by seemingly everyone to be archaic, restrictive, and not trendy, to say the least. Where did this important, good "chutzpah" go? When did we decide it was no longer useful? The archetype of the meek, unsure *baal teshuvah* is unfortunate. Our communities are lacking because of it. But, most importantly, the individual *baal/baalas teshuvah* is the most negatively impacted of all.

In *Pirkei Avos* it says: "Who is wise? One who learns from all people."[7] The *Rishonim* go out of their way to point out that this applies even to those less knowledgeable or of a lesser spiritual stature than oneself.[8] The world at large, despite its inability to act as a moral compass, does possess areas of valuable knowledge and skill, as the Midrash states: "*Chochmah b'goyim ta'amin*—there is wisdom among the nations."[9] Those who have been placed in the secular world by Hashem but who, through their search for *emes*, have chosen a Torah life are often the very people who can act as conduits to uplift the information they absorbed and the experiences they had in their lives, through positive contribution to their families and communities.

Relating to Secular Family and Friends

Along with developing a healthy self-perception, it is equally vital to develop healthy relationships with secular family and friends. It is crucial to make a distinction between not *frum* and not healthy. The two are completely different, and this distinction should inform subsequent

---

7   *Pirkei Avos* 4:1.
8   *Rashi; Bartenura; Machzor Vitri; Rabbeinu Yonah.*
9   *Eichah Rabbah* 2:13.

behaviors and mindsets when dealing with family or specific situations. Dysfunction within an individual or family unit may limit the degree to which an individual should ideally be involved with those family members. For the purposes of this book, we will be addressing the relationship between the *baal/baalas teshuvah* and his/her secular family assuming an underlying healthy dynamic. Where there is an unhealthy family dynamic, it is important to receive personalized guidance from *daas Torah* on how to best deal with each specific situation.

Hashem created a parent-child system as a window into our relationship with Him. Our parents provide for us, give of their love and resources, and raise us with values to the best of their abilities. They shape our personalities and our sense of self. Unlike God, our parents are human and they therefore inherently possess weaknesses and flaws. We have to be able to understand these flaws while simultaneously showing gratitude for everything they have given us. Being secular is almost never the flaw of any parent. The majority of parents and other family members of *baalei teshuvah* never had a real choice in whether they were observant or not, due to their lack of exposure, education, and many other factors.

The overarching focus in our relationships with family should be on fulfilling *kibbud av v'eim* and maintaining positive relationships without compromising our values. The more secure a person is in their own observance and Jewish identity, the easier it will be to strike this balance. It is possible, and necessary, to respect a person without condoning or agreeing with their behaviors. Many in society today disagree with this notion. We are constantly sent the message that unless we can condone and even congratulate a person's behavior, we cannot have a positive and warm relationship with that individual. A Torah perspective maintains a different approach. In the laws of *tochachah*,[10] offering criticism for someone's wrongdoing is actually prohibited unless we are able to ascertain that the *mussar* may be accepted. We are told that the Torah's ways are pleasant, *"Deracheha darchei noam."*[11] We can and should find

---

10   *Yevamos* 65b and *Nimukei Yosef* ibid.
11   *Mishlei* 3:17.

traits and characteristics of our family members that we respect, and express our admiration of these. Our new life should not be a message of rejection of all the gifts we were given by our parents and family members throughout our lives, and certainly not of the people themselves.

> *A newly observant couple attended a wedding of a relative where they saw many old friends and acquaintances. They barely said hello to the individuals with whom they had in the past spent many hours and had close relationships. Understandably, these people were quite put off by the "way that becoming religious" changed their former friends.*

This is a shame because it is a missed opportunity to make a *kiddush Hashem*: on the one hand, by showing that a Torah personality is friendly and warm, and at the same time not compromising on any values or standards.

A positive example:

> *A young woman who was growing in her Jewish observance in high school would often remind her parents, "It's not despite of you that I'm becoming religious, it's because of you!" And she would go on to list the traits her parents had instilled in her that sparked her journey. She would point out their value of critical thinking, of inspiration, of intellectual honesty. These parents certainly felt that they were a valued part of her journey even when her life choices differed from theirs.*

Sharing Is Caring

Often, a person who has found truth and meaning in his/her own life is enthusiastic about sharing it with those closest to them. This person needs to understand that a warm, respectful, and positive relationship will do more in making a positive impression of Judaism on our family than unsolicited "teaching." If we find ourselves spending Shabbos in the home of our secular family, it is far more beneficial and impactful to invest time and energy in making Shabbos dinner and inviting any family who would like to join rather than berating parents and siblings for turning the lights on and off. People naturally respond with interest to learning about things toward which they feel positive. Cultivate a positive impression of Judaism and Jewish life and you may find you have a far more captivated audience with whom to share Torah ideas than if you attempt to create a school classroom out of family gatherings and interactions.

Why We Sometimes Respond Negatively

Frequently, we will respond in a negative manner to secular family and friends in moments of insecurity. If we find ourselves in a situation where the people around us are not speaking or behaving in ways that are consistent with our level of observance or values, it is expected that we may notice this and feel inwardly uncomfortable. Through a Torah lifestyle, we have developed sensitivities to many aspects of life—speech, eating, Shabbos, and male/female dynamics, among many others. We may feel like the lenses on our glasses have been cleaned and our vision is sharper, more developed. But these sensitivities are not enough to warrant negative or insulting comments toward people who simply do not know any better and with whom we seek to maintain positive, long-term relationships. Instead, we should do some soul-searching to discover why we feel frustrated or offended by others' behaviors to such a great degree. Often, we will find that it is because of something lacking within ourselves, not them, that is causing such an intense, unsettled feeling. Is it my own recent entry into observance or my limited knowledge about the mitzvos I've taken on? Or do I feel insecure about how different I look from everyone else? Perhaps there are family dynamics that trigger self-doubt? Suddenly, we realize that

- it's not their *treif* food that really bothers me but my seemingly over-simplified understanding of why I need the special kosher food on my plate;
- it's not my sister's pants that make me feel indignant but rather my feeling of awkward newness in wearing the skirt I chose to commit to;

- it's not my parent's lack of Shabbos observance that frustrates me; instead, it is unresolved feelings about my beliefs not being taken seriously.

In the spaces in our lives where we feel truly secure, we may experience intellectual disagreement with others and even feel passionate about our stance, but we will rarely be overwhelmed by an emotional feeling of opposition or frustration with those who do not do and think as we do. Once we arrive at the true root of the issue, we can begin to remedy the problem, fill our void, and establish greater inner peace and confidence. This will allow us to engage with others in a calm and pleasant way.

This also often happens when we are faced with questions from friends and family and we are caught off guard or don't feel equipped with the "right" answer. We tend to envision the "right" answer to be the one that inspires the person in front of us to embark on a path of Torah observance. This is naive and puts unnecessary pressure on our interactions with people. Our own sense of happiness and fulfillment will make a deeper impression on those around us than any particular answer, brilliant or witty as it may be. When a person asks us a question about our lifestyle, values, or particular behaviors, it is our job to give a sincere and thoughtful response that addresses the issues to the best of our abilities. If we find that we do not know the answer or explanation to a sincere question, it is an opportunity to research and find out for both the friend who inquired and for ourselves. The ability to articulate an idea is the first indicator of one's degree of understanding it in the first place.

However, it is important to be aware of an all-too-common pitfall. Many times, we encounter what seems to be a question that is in fact not a question at all but rather a statement. Often, a statement is disguised in the form of a question. Ask yourself: *Is this person truly seeking information or open to new ideas? Or are they trying to criticize or tear down my lifestyle and/or value system?* It behooves one to learn to recognize the difference between a question (?) and a question (!). Many times, a question (!) can be avoided or dealt with via humor or a change of topic and need not make one feel defensive. In fact, best practice is to avoid directly answering a statement that is being disguised as a question.

I would bet that every observant woman with secular family and acquaintances has been asked the following during the summer months: "It's so hot outside, aren't you *so* hot in all those clothes?" and periodically, "So, how many babies are you actually planning to have?" Nine out of ten times, neither of these questions are expressions of a sincere quest for the Jewish approach to modesty or family. Nor are they expressions of sympathy or support. Rather, such questions often come with undertones of mockery and preconceived conclusions about the irrationality of religious life. Therefore, they are best responded to with anything that conveys the message that we are, in fact, rational people who are happy and secure with the lifestyle decisions we have made. Often, letting our curious friend know that they "will be the first to know when I decide to have my next baby" is exactly the response they need to find their "question" answered.

> *A young woman had recently come back from a year in seminary and was attending a relative's bat mitzvah party. The party, for which she had received personalized guidance from her rabbi about attending and how she should handle various halachic issues that would arise there, was held in a treif restaurant with a large dance floor and a DJ. When everyone went to dance in between eating, it quickly became apparent that she was not joining. Several people at the party came up to her and, in pitying tones, asked if it was really true that she could no longer have fun and dance like everyone else. She smiled sweetly and responded, "I really don't feel like dancing with twelve-year-olds, you know what I mean?" They had nothing to say. She wasn't rude or condescending. And she wasn't preachy. She portrayed confidence and satisfaction in her decision and made a joke out of the situation. Later that evening, one of the people from that group came over to her and quietly asked to know more about why she wasn't dancing. This time she felt the sincerity of the woman's question and they proceeded to have a friendly and positive conversation about the new values and standards she had incorporated into her life and how meaningful these were to her.*

Always know what you are answering when a question is thrown your way. Consider whether a real question underlies the words and phrases being said. This will help guide your response to be both respectful and dignified.

It's Worth It

Positive relationships with family members and others from our past are an opportunity to show appropriate gratitude to the people who gave to us and cared for us, and, in so doing, to create *kiddush Hashem* in the world. They also build our internal awareness that Hashem's decision regarding our background and upbringing was purposeful and inherently positive. In the end, no one will care for us, love us, and support us quite like our family. These relationships are worth great personal investment to maintain and to strengthen. And through this, we create a significantly better, healthier, and more pleasant environment into which we bring our children.

Asei Lecha Rav:
What Does This Really Mean and How Do We Do It

I n *Pirkei Avos*, Chazal instruct us: *"Asei lecha rav,"*[12] literally translated as "Make for yourself a teacher." The vast majority of *baalei teshuvah* developed a connection to Torah through a teacher who exposed them not only to Torah facts and ideas but opened a doorway into the values, ideals, and life of a Torah Jew. One cannot expect to continue growing and thriving as Torah-true Jews without a continued connection to a Torah teacher. In light of the critical role their rabbi or teacher has played in helping them reach their commitment to Torah and mitzvos, *baalei teshuvah* typically have an internal sense for how true this is, sometimes even more so than their FFB (*frum* from birth) counterparts. Still, the nature and depth of this statement needs to be

---

12   *Pirkei Avos* 1:6.

fully explored, as a deep and nuanced understanding of this topic is crucial to one's spiritual well-being and success.

Torah is not meant to be studied like an encyclopedic piece of literature. Judaism is not meant to be experienced while living in isolation. This is the concept of the Oral Torah and the requirement for teacher-student relationships in order for the Jewish nation as a whole to survive, as well as for each individual Jew. The structure of Judaism is such that there is a built-in need for a *rav*, a teacher throughout life, regardless of one's level of scholarship, knowledge, or experience. Thus, even great Torah scholars and leaders always had rabbis themselves, whom they turned to for wisdom and guidance.

The *sefer Lada'as Ba'aretz Darkecha*[13] explains that in order to have a deep connection with Torah, it is a prerequisite to have a close relationship with a true *talmid chacham*. The depth of Torah is such that many of the ideas and concepts of proper Torah life are difficult to convey with words, and there is therefore no way to be sure we understand how to live Torah life if we do not observe the behavior of great rabbis and rebbetzins as much as possible, in as many different situations as we can. The Talmud relates that Rabbi Yehuda HaNasi said: "I would not have merited to understand the Torah if I had not gazed upon the back of Rabbi Meir."[14] Words can only encapsulate the "*chomer*" of Torah, the basic ideas. But the main component of true wisdom, "*tzurah*," the sensitivity of the heart as it gains understanding—referred to as *nishmas haTorah* (the soul of the Torah)—cannot be contained in words. Instead, the deep desire of the wise person to share his wisdom with others explodes outward from his being, expressing itself in his every movement. When the student watches the teacher during the lesson and in his day-to-day life, his heart connects with the heart of his teacher and understands the unspoken words and thoughts emanating from the heart of his teacher. He connects to the Torah teachings as they express themselves in real life through a person who has integrated

---

13   Yehuda Greenwald, *Lada'as Ba'aretz Darkecha, Pirkei Hadrachah L'Baalei Teshuvah* (Jerusalem, 1996), p. 170.

14   *Yerushalmi Beitzah* 5:2

these into his personality and daily routine. This is why if someone were to live in total seclusion, studying Torah texts in an exhaustive manner, and would one day decide to rejoin society, he or she would not emerge looking and acting like a Torah Jew—despite potentially great levels of scholarship. This is because this person never saw, through personal example, how to apply Torah wisdom and direction to real living in any particular time or place. The built-in requirement for a relationship with a Torah teacher is what allows the Torah to be a "living," eternally applicable guidebook.

What Makes the Right "Rav" for You?

- He needs to be a *talmid chacham*—someone with vast Torah knowledge that comes from a connection to *mesorah*, the transmission of that knowledge from one generation of Torah scholars to the next.
- He should be a role model of upright character and refined personal behavior.
- He needs to be able to understand you. His personal background does not have to mirror yours, but he needs to be able to positively relate to where you are coming from and where you are today and the details that shaped and colored that journey. If he cannot relate to you individually and see your unique background as a positive factor in your development, his guidance could even be counterproductive. He must understand that who you are today is not disconnected from your past but a very integral part of it. These qualities may be easier to find in a *rav* who is highly experienced in guiding *baalei teshuvah*.
- A personal rabbi needs to be accessible. I have often heard from students: "I have a great, wise, inspiring rabbi from seminary in Israel but it's so hard to reach him." If he cannot be a regular, consistent part of your life, he will not have the context or up-to-date information required to give you relevant guidance or answers to your questions. Of course, one can—and should!—maintain a relationship with such a rabbi, but at the same time should be careful to set realistic expectations for

the ways in which they can benefit therefrom. For example, inspiration, general encouragement, and perspective on broad philosophical topics are all important ways in which such a relationship can continue to play an important role in this individual's life. Meanwhile, one should seek out a local or otherwise more accessible *rav* who will be capable of giving guidance in more personal or complex areas.

The Nature of This Relationship

What we have discussed so far brings to light the issues of the nature of this teacher/student relationship. What are the dynamics and parameters of this relationship? Is Chazal's instruction to create a connection to one particular rabbi, or is it referencing an entire category of people who play a vital role in our spiritual development and well-being? How do we create this kind of relationship, and how do we utilize it correctly?

A reasonable person understands that in order to maintain physical health it is imperative to find a competent doctor and see him regularly in order to check the continued maintenance of their health and to consult with when health-related questions and concerns arise. To take this analogy a step further, consider the fact that doctors specialize in specific areas. For their annual check-up, a person visits their internist. But foot pain will lead them to contact a podiatrist; digestion-related problems, a gastroenterologist; heart problems, a cardiologist; and so on and so forth.

When it comes to our rabbis and teachers, we observe a similar phenomenon. We need to seek specialized individuals and responses depending on the topic or nature of the issue for which we seek guidance. And just as a doctor will require holistic knowledge of our current health, our health history, and even family health history in order to provide the best care, so too a rabbi needs to be able to understand not only who we are today but how we developed and the broader background from which we come.

Halachah questions, *hadrachah* or *eitzah*, and a request for a *berachah* are all different reasons to approach a teacher or rabbi. But the very different nature of each of these and their expected outcomes will significantly impact who we ask and the results of that interaction. Just as you wouldn't call your accountant about your foot pain, a rabbi is not a *navi*, magician, or all-encompassing go-to person. A *posek*, *gadol*, personal *rav*, and mentor all hold different positions and are meant to be engaged differently.

A Psak Halachah

A *posek* is a rabbi who specializes in areas of Jewish law. He may also be our personal rabbi, but that's not a prerequisite to consult him. A response to a question of Jewish law is binding and must be adhered to unless we present the original answer we received to another rabbi and receive explicit permission to do otherwise. Asking a halachic *sh'eilah* is much like deciding on a country to move to. We have many options of countries in the world. Some are socialist states, some operate under communist regimes, and some are democratic. We may pick a country that reflects our values and stances on many aspects of life. But once we move there, we are subject to their system of law. We understand that we are expected to be law-abiding citizens, regardless of the fact that we had the freedom to choose to settle there. This concept applies similarly to questions of Jewish law.

We should think carefully about which rabbi best reflects our *hashkafah*—our philosophical outlook and flavor within Torah Judaism—and possesses a general understanding of our background and broad knowledge of Jewish law. He need not be a *baal teshuvah* himself or have attended university, but he should be capable of relating to who we are and see our background in a nonjudgmental light. Once we receive a halachic answer, our behavior should reflect the awareness that this is binding for us personally. The system of Jewish law is broad but also requires adherence to its standards, much like a country demands its citizens to keep its laws.

Of course, it may take many interactions with different rabbis in this category to find the one we feel most comfortable approaching. On one hand, a *psak* from a *rav* may make us stretch our comfort zones, gently pushing us to new levels of growth. This is inherently positive, as it holds great potential for our Jewish growth. On the other hand, if we find that the *psakim* we are receiving on a regular basis feel out of line with who we are or our personal *derech*, it is appropriate to seek out another *rav* whose approach to *psak halachah* will resonate with us. Arriving at this balance will be a process. Our patience and willingness to engage proactively here will build a deeper understanding of ourselves as well as this vital relationship.

A Request for a Berachah

It is popular to ask for a blessing from a *gadol* or great person among the Jewish people. This could be a very positive experience. Asking for a blessing is a form of supplication to the Almighty. A person who has achieved greatness in Torah scholarship and personal development certainly has a power of prayer that exceeds most. Their prayers on your behalf carry great weight with Hashem. Additionally, the experience of meeting a person who embodies Torah is impactful and inspiring on its own. As long as we keep in mind that a *gadol* does not possess *nevuah*, and, consequently, without a close relationship with you cannot give personalized answers to very specific questions in a way that will be productive and relevant on an individual level, the experience of meeting a *gadol* and receiving a *berachah* is almost always positive and worthwhile.

Seeking Hadrachah

Seeking *hadrachah* or *eitzah*, advice and guidance, can be a far more complex and broad process than either a halachic *sh'eilah* or request for a *berachah*. Torah wisdom can be found in a variety of places within the Jewish community. This can include, but is not limited to, a rabbi, rebbetzin, teacher, neighbor who is a stage or two ahead of us in life and who we look up to, or other role-model figure. A personal rabbi or mentor should ideally have an in-depth understanding of our background and the nuances of our lives. Their responses to us will only be helpful and benefit us to the degree to which we are honest about the entirety of the situations or dilemmas we present. Their responses are also not binding in the same way as those pertaining to Jewish law.

When we go for advice or guidance about a particular situation, it is important that we are careful not to outsource our own thinking or intuition to another person. In these instances, the mentor's input is meant to inform, enlighten, and broaden our perspective through their great wisdom and life experience, but without dictating exactly what we are to do with the guidance we receive. It is best to avoid the temptation to "hand off" our difficulties to the rabbi or mentor, passing along our questions without properly thinking them through.

Particularly when asking for guidance (a non-halachic question), we should ideally first weigh the issue carefully and develop our own thoughts about what the correct path is. Then, we should present the entire issue, describing all angles of the question. The rabbi or teacher can then respond to help us clarify if our approach to the issue was correct. What we decide to do with the advice given in any situation may impact our lives significantly, and only we will bear the responsibility of the decisions we make and their outcomes. If we ask for guidance in dating, we should give serious consideration to the feedback we receive, but we must remember that no one will have to marry this person but us. No one will live with them or be required to build a life with them. It is us, and only us, who will ultimately be taking this upon ourselves. Therefore, while it may be far easier to simply be "told what to do," we cannot expect such responses to our questions and dilemmas.

A baalas teshuvah, frum for several years, had been dating for some time when she felt that she might have met the man who would be her husband. She approached her rabbi for feedback on some of the strengths and weakness of this young man. She felt she needed clarity in processing the various aspects of their relationship, as well as how this individual compared to the vision she had of what would make a good match for her. Her rabbi helped to refocus her thought process on what was most important for her in a spouse. He also asked important, thought-provoking questions about the young man and what their life together might be like. And finally, he reminded the young woman that he could never decide for her whether or not she should marry a particular person. The young woman left with some very important questions answered, and even more to give serious thought to.

Years later, she looks back at this conversation with immense gratitude. The guidance and support of her rabbi, who knew her well and pushed her to higher levels of self-awareness, allowed her to make many conscious, small decisions about this person and what she really needed in her marriage. She feels that the things this conversation led her to think through, accept, and evaluate enabled her to not only marry the young man but to successfully handle the various challenges that came up in their marriage over the years.

This can be contrasted with the following less positive scenario.

A baalas teshuvah, unhappily married for almost ten years, looks back at her dating process and bemoans the pressure she received from involved parties to marry that particular young man. It was, she feels, a mistake.

However, at the end of the day, she needed to realize that the burden of responsibility for the decision whether or not to marry him was hers to make, and that she alone would bear the consequences. This is regardless of the fact that support and guidance in such a critical decision were quite necessary.

A young man in his early twenties had been studying in yeshiva for several years and felt settled in his observant life. He approached his rabbi for guidance on what his next steps should be. He could remain in yeshiva for a longer duration. He could return to his hometown in America. He could pursue his career in either location. There were many options and he felt overwhelmed by the major life consequences of these decisions. He spoke with his rabbi a number of times, going through the various options, their possible impact on his life, and his own feelings on what would be best for him. After each meeting, the young man emerged with much to think about and also with more clarity and wisdom than he had possessed initially. Eventually, he made the decision to spend some more time in yeshiva before returning to the States later that year to continue his studies toward his eventual career. He looks back at these interactions as some of his most developmental and expansive experiences.

Alternatively, lacking such positively impactful experiences can affect our lives for the long term.

A man who returned to observance in his late teens and is now in his fifties speaks bitterly about his inability to support his family after having spent twenty years in kollel and constantly being discouraged to leave or find alternate means of livelihood.

Life-altering decisions that steer us in a particular direction, and the significant details and factors that shape such decisions, require serious thought and often a lot of input from those greater than us. However, in the end, the decisions we make and their subsequent impact on us and our families is our responsibility. We will be built up from guidance received in this manner. It will enable us to carry our challenges, successes, and even failures in a capable and dignified way.

A mother of several young children approached her seminary teacher for her perspectives on tzniyus in the household. She chose to speak to this particular teacher because she knew her well and the teacher reflected the standards and ideals she sought to instill in her own home. After spending time speaking through her thoughts on the topic, the woman's teacher shared her perspectives of tzniyus within the family and some of the practical things she does in her home. She made sure to emphasize that she was not sharing halachah, but rather personal practices that stem from her understanding and integration of this particular topic.

This baalas teshuvah mother gained valuable insights from a person she respected and viewed as her role model. She had a sense of some of the practical ways in which someone she aspired to be like actually lived tzniyus. Following this conversation, she decided to implement a few of the ideas her teacher mentioned. Other ideas were not what she felt she could incorporate into her life at that moment. She felt empowered.

Often, we will feel most confident in our life choices when we combine the wisdom we receive from our rabbis and mentors with our inner voice. Our great teachers know how to guide us toward achieving this balance.

I attended a seminary where the overwhelming majority of girls had Hebrew names. Before long, my friend and I found ourselves in our principal's office inquiring whether or not we should start going by our Hebrew names—even though these were not the ones we were given at birth or called by with family and friends. He took the time to explain the significance of a Hebrew name. He mentioned the fact it was listed as one of three reasons that the Jews were redeemed from Egypt and the idea that one's Hebrew name reflects their essence and purpose in the world, among others. And he also took care to say that it is not mandatory to be called by one's Hebrew name, that if it causes "World War III" at home it might not be the most important battle to fight right now. My friend left that meeting as "Chana Malka" and I left as "Jenny." The beauty is that we were both right. We both made informed decisions that resonated with each of us.

Sometimes, we need to get advice from someone we trust—even if only to validate what we "sense inside" is true:

A young woman with whom I had a close relationship approached me after class one day and asked for my thoughts on whether she should go back to spend more time in seminary. She had gone the previous year and there were people in her life who told her it was imperative that she go back for a longer period of time. We discussed the idea and weighed the pros and cons. She shared that she felt a deeper degree of growth

since settling into a Torah-observant community than she
did in seminary. She felt she needed to take more advantage
of learning opportunities in her community but that she was
overall on a positive trajectory. While I gave input, she came to
the conclusion that fit her best.

One of the greatest gifts of a wise rabbi or teacher is their ability to
know when to answer our questions and when to hold off on an immediate
response and instead encourage further discussion on the topic at hand.

A recent baalas teshuvah attended an oneg at the home of a
family that worked in outreach. It was her first time meeting the
family and attending an event in their home. After the oneg, she
approached the rabbi and rebbetzin and asked if they thought she
should relocate for dating. The couple responded with the only
responsible answer possible—"We don't know." They encouraged
her to set a time to meet with them so they could get to know her,
understand the context within which she was asking her question,
and talk through possibilities for the best course of action.

These are all nuanced situations that benefit from perspective but
not necessarily from absolute directives.

In his commentary to the Mishnah in *Avos* that we quoted above, Rabbi
Avraham J. Twerski mentions that just as it is important to have a mentor
and teacher, it is also important not to lose one's sense of self and to realize
that we must exercise our own capacity for judgement as well. He says,

Ultimately, a person is responsible for his own judgments.
In matters of halachah, we must defer to the acknowledged
authority. We must also set our own opinion aside even in
non-halachic issues if we are specifically instructed to do so by a
competent Torah authority. However, we must be careful that
we maintain a reasonable attitude of self-reliance.[15]

---

15   Rabbi Abraham J. Twerski, MD, *Visions of the Fathers* (New York: Shaar Press, 2009), p. 32.

To this end, he tells the story of a person he knew who always consulted his rebbe as to which name to give a newborn child. One time he came to the rebbe and handed him a *kvittel*, where he listed all his children by name except for the youngest daughter, who was four months old.

"What is your daughter's name?" the rebbe asked.

"I haven't yet named her," the man replied. "When she was born, I sent a message to the rebbe asking what name to give her, and since I didn't receive a reply, I haven't named her yet." The rebbe was not happy!

> *A young family attended a Shabbos meal where both mother and father hesitated to participate in the lively conversation, save for an occasional quote from their rabbis. They reasoned that any independent thoughts or ideas that included their own insights may be influenced by the yetzer hara, so it would be safer to abstain from acknowledging or sharing these.*
>
> *One of the other people at the meal noted that it seemed ironic that they had been able to find their way to the light and truth of Torah and God, but from then on it was their yetzer hara that reigned over them.*

The guest was pointing out that even while the guidance and input of those who possess more Torah knowledge and insight is essential, the *daas*, insight, and thinking of a *baal* or *baalas teshuvah* is what led them to *emes*. There is no reason to distrust its abilities to inform subsequent decisions made in life.

Often, our rabbis will guide us in developing our own decision-making abilities.

> *A young man, frum for many years, would frequently consult a rebbi from his yeshiva, with whom he had a close relationship, about major life decisions. Since their relationship spanned a number of years, this man came to expect that just after he would present his situation to his rebbi, the almost-instant reply would be, "OK, and what do you think you should do?"*

While this was at times difficult to hear, and what he would have loved was to be told what the best course of action would be, this young man came to appreciate the invaluable experience of processing his thoughts with someone wiser and greater than himself.

Change Can Be Difficult

Often, *baalei teshuvah* feel frustrated that the rabbis and rebbetzins with whom they initially explored Judaism and began their journey to observance seem less available to them than they once were. This is not intentional. Often, it is the result of the technical difficulties in keeping up with former students and simultaneously meeting the expectations of their employers to bring in, teach, and connect with new students.

Furthermore, when we think of it objectively, we often see that those who introduced us to this path are not necessarily the most fit to take us further along it. Perhaps the community we have chosen or the ideological outlooks we have developed differ from those of our initial teachers. Since we are looking for personalized guidance, we will acquire it to a greater degree from those who reflect our general *hashkafah*. It could also be that our first rabbi and/or rebbetzin do not possess the life experience required to give us the guidance we need in our current place in life. For instance, if we met this family on a college campus, then it is likely that their primary area of expertise is in guiding students during their college years. They may not have enough experience with providing guidance to families with young children who are dealing with the school system or other aspects of life within their community of choice, and for providing the insights needed at this point. Instead of feeling isolated and unsupported in one's continued growth and development, one has to proactively seek out and create new relationships that will address these very important needs.

A baalas teshuvah who recently moved into the frum community in her city made sure to make new connections by eating Shabbos meals at the homes of different families whenever the opportunity presented itself. At one such meal she noticed how warm and welcoming this particular family was. She felt she had much in common with them: they had become frum many years earlier and seemed to uphold the values she hoped to imbue into her future home. She volunteered to help out if they ever needed babysitting or an extra hand in cooking for Shabbos. By spending more and more time with this family and forming a close relationship with the mother in particular, she found that she had an address for many of the questions she had about integrating into the frum community and how to create the Jewish home she longed for.

Often, if we put in the effort and have an open mind we will find the resources we are looking for.

A young man, emerging from several years of introductory Jewish study, was searching for more in-depth learning and was looking to experience life within an established Jewish community. That year, as he helped clean homes for Pesach, as was common for yeshiva bachurim to do, he met a particular family whose father gave shiurim in his community. He went to several of this rabbi's classes and was so inspired by him that he decided to enroll in the yeshiva where this rabbi taught. This was the beginning of a relationship that would be a source of guidance for years to come and in the various stages of life that would ensue.

If we seek out information from appropriate sources, we can avoid situations where we deal with our questions in less-than-ideal ways.

A mother of several young children found herself inquiring of her eight-year-old son's friends about the bedtime routines in their respective homes. Her sense of insecurity in running a Torah-observant household led to her trying to fill this void through self-denigrating means. This is unnecessary and coun-terproductive for both the mother and her children.

We must be proactive in establishing the support system we need to function optimally:

- Attending *shiurim* given by rabbis and teachers in the community who seem like possible candidates for connection is a great way to develop new relationships.
- Asking friends or acquaintances to suggest individuals in the community who are available and possess Torah wisdom we might benefit from is another way to develop awareness of the resources that are available in our community.
- When attending a Shabbos meal at the home of a neighbor or family in the community, we should be on the lookout for and make note of any admirable traits and behaviors. When questions regarding *chinuch* or family routines come up in conversation, we can ask for feedback and insights.

It is possible to find sources of guidance to fuel our continued growth within the community. It doesn't mean that our initial relationships need to be purposely dropped—but they can certainly be supplemented as needed.

Too Many Cooks in the Kitchen

At the same time, we want to avoid creating a *hadrachah* runaround—with too many chefs in the kitchen, so to speak. If we ask too many people for their input on a situation, we will be gathering too many varied perspectives and approaches. As a result, we may find ourselves in a state of confusion, more hindered than strengthened. On a deeper level, a person who runs from person to person seeking advice must ask himself if he is truly seeking advice or an escape. Are they running from something within themselves that they know they would have to confront through a truly close connection with a mentor who knows them very well? If we are honestly looking for personalized guidance in any given area, we will not have to survey dozens of people on the issue before arriving at the wisdom we need. Rather, we will likely have to confront ourselves in deep ways that require strength and bravery because it is through our questions and our struggles that we also uncover the weaker parts of ourselves and have the potential to strengthen them. Ideally, one should identify several key people who embody the Torah values and ideals they strive for and with whom they can develop a close connection. They will then be able to approach them as various issues come up that would benefit from guidance and input.

Hadrachah in the Digital Age

As social media grows in popularity and frequency of use, it becomes necessary to address just one of its many limitations and pitfalls. There are many people who turn to social media forums for advice on highly personal and often nuanced life situations. You will certainly not find *daas Torah* on social media! It's questionable whether one can even find wisdom that will be beneficial to their specific question or challenge there either.

Of course, it is much easier to post a question for hundreds, if not thousands, of strangers to respond to rather than investing the real time, emotional energy, and honesty it takes to form a real connection with a rabbi or mentor who will be able to give us tailored guidance. However, the risks are quite great as well. We do not know the people who respond to us. Making assumptions about who a person is and their qualifications based on an online persona that they have created is often unwise. We have no idea of the flawed perspectives due to personal struggles and issues that may accompany people's responses on the internet. Often people walk away from engaging in a string of advice-giving on social media platforms carrying not only their own issues but those of dozens of others as well. Furthermore, when people give advice online, they walk away from that interaction bearing virtually no *achrayus*, true responsibility, for the impact they may have on another person. A real mentor will always feel the burden of influencing another person's life in potentially significant ways. This will ensure that they give careful thought and proper focus to the feedback and guidance they impart.

Becoming an Informed Consumer

We must be cognizant of the fact that there are many who enjoy giving advice to others, and especially to *baalei teshuvah*, who often lack family input and support with regard to seminary or yeshiva, dating, school choices for children, and other important life experiences and decisions that are an integral part of observant life. This can be well-intentioned, but we must ensure that we are informed consumers of this advice and from whom we receive it. We should choose our mentors and teachers actively rather than being passive recipients of other people's thoughts and perspectives. We need to make sure that we have selected individuals to be role models of the type of life and values we aspire to, that they possess the wisdom we seek, and whom we have determined will add value to the current question or life situation we face.

The Big Picture

Ultimately, we have to take responsibility for ourselves, and our Yiddishkeit becomes an expression of that responsibility. In this way, we have the opportunity to develop our confidence and self-reliance, which will prove invaluable as tools for handling everything that comes our way in life and everything we will do as a result. While a relationship with a rabbi is a central aspect in leading a Torah life, he does not have to be the address for every type of question or the finalizing point of approval on every decision reached. Just as the doctor serves as a resource to inform and raise awareness of the proper maintenance of our health, we must learn how to remain spiritually healthy as we utilize the various experts in our lives to further our spiritual growth.

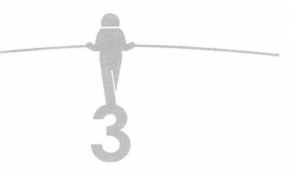

Limud HaTorah:
Nourishment for the Soul

n *Mishlei*,[16] Shlomo HaMelech outlines the ultimate principle in growth and education. He instructs: *"Chanoch l'naar al pi darko."* The classic understanding of this verse is for parents and teachers: just as each child is an individual with unique needs and abilities, so too should his education be customized to have the deepest and most productive impact on him. Rabbi Avigdor Miller, one of the *gedolei Yisrael* of the previous generation, quotes the Alter of Slabodka as adding a dimension to this understanding of the verse. The Alter, Rabbi Miller says, would teach that this verse also addresses those people whose parents did not give them the education required. He says they must guide themselves on a lifelong path of growth and development. Essentially, we are our own child as well. We have a responsibility to educate, train, and develop our "inner child."

---

16   *Mishlei* 22:6.

At the core of this process is the development of a Torah mindset. Everyone has a lens through which they view and evaluate the world, and upon which they base their decisions. We need to seek and acquire clarity of vision through a Torah lens. This will form the center of our worldview, personal goals, and both major and minor life decisions. Many well-intentioned secular Jews dispute the necessity of mitzvah observance by claiming they are "Jewish at heart." We must question—what does it mean to have a Jewish heart? The heart symbolizes the motivation and impetus behind our actions. If our actions are not Jewish actions, our heart may lack Jewish ideals and passion. A Jewish heart by definition leads to a Jewish life. And an active Jewish life, in turn, is meant to build and develop a Jewish heart. The two are inextricably intertwined.

The key to developing a Jewish heart, as well as a Jewish mindset, is Torah learning. From the dawn of our history as a nation, the centrality of learning in defining Jewish life, outlook, and identity has proven axiomatic. Our enemies have always known the key to our survival as Jews is our connection to Torah and our ability to engage in its study. The Torah informs our identity and our personal and national purpose in the world. Without an understanding of who we are, where we come from, and the implications of this knowledge on our daily lives, we are subject to assimilation and spiritual death. It is not a coincidence that the ancient Greeks outlawed Torah study when pleasant invitations to participate in public events and assemblies failed to achieve the intended goal of assimilation. When Torah scholars and Torah scrolls were burned in ancient Rome and in medieval Europe, it was not a purely symbolic act; it was a deep awareness that the Torah was the key to our identity. In more recent history, Jews who emigrated from the former Soviet Union found that they lacked even the basic Jewish facts and cultural knowledge possessed by their American counterparts who had received it as part and parcel of their upbringing. As a result, their Jewish practice and observance was correspondingly less than even the minimal levels common among their American neighbors.

In fact, almost all *baalei teshuvah* likely come from backgrounds with little Jewish knowledge. Without fundamental Torah knowledge and continued learning, we end up with "cut-flower Judaism." It is pretty—but disconnected from the roots and can therefore not reproduce nor be sustained. Examples include various forms of cultural or non-Orthodox Judaism, which relied on traditional foods, holidays, attending synagogue on high holidays, and periodic transmission of some cultural relics and vague morals as their sole expressions of Judaism. We who came from a cut-flower Judaism reconnected to the root through Torah learning, which led to Torah action. Our friends and peers who did not are sadly unlikely to identify as Jews in the long run. Over time, the pretty flower will finally wilt and waste away.

We prioritize Torah learning and education as the keys to developing and sustaining our lives as Torah Jews. Learning creates *daas*. *Daas* is a type of knowledge or understanding that implies total connection. Just as Adam and Chavah in Gan Eden experienced a total and exclusive connection—as the verse says: *"V'ha'adam yada es Chavah ishto"*[17]—*daas* implies more than the learning of facts; it is the bridge between knowing intellectually and connecting to that knowledge with one's entire being. Torah study creates *daas*, the bridge between the individual Jew and his or her Jewish life.

Different Types of Learning

There is an important distinction that must be made when discussing Torah learning. There is a difference between inspiration and the acquiring of knowledge. Everyone needs inspiration, excitement, "fluff." But this will not translate into internalizing a mindset that will affect our everyday lives. Just as a vacation is to rejuvenate in order to come back to real life with more vigor and readiness to be productive, so too a large, well-attended shiur on a topic of broad interest and appeal is meant to excite, enliven, and motivate us, but the goal of all this should be to go back to our real work with greater dedication.

One can hear amazing marketing about an incredible medical school program—the students from this program will become the next

---

17   *Bereishis* 4:1.

generation's top medical professionals, many professional doors will be open to its graduates, and students will have access to support from the most respected professionals in the field, the most updated research and information available in all areas of medicine. But until you enroll, go to class, and study for the exams, you will not know anything about medicine and you will certainly not become a doctor.

I frequently ask the women who attend my classes to estimate how many people would come to a class advertised as a *shalom bayis* course. They give an educated guess that if it is given in a large community with a popular speaker, one can expect around fifty or more attendees. Now, I ask them, how many people would you estimate coming to a weekly parashah class? They reply—perhaps five or six. Life experience shows this estimate to be accurate. It is interesting because if every husband were to emulate the character traits of Avraham Avinu and every wife were to learn from the ways of Sarah Imeinu, it can be argued that marriages would be greatly enhanced by the giving and kind nature, the good *middos*, and the other-centered perspectives that would suddenly be infused into the relationship on a regular basis. Of course, *shalom bayis* classes are important, and maintaining a successful marriage is a complex endeavor. Still, one should never forget that prepackaged ideas can never substitute personal acquisition of information and ideas. Rav Hirsch says that "life as lived should be the flower of knowledge."[18] It is the knowledge we acquire as Torah students that will inform and construct the basis of our lives.

Torah is both the heritage and the obligation of every Jew, no matter how old we are or how knowledgeable we are or aren't.

> *A recently married baalas teshuvah was proudly giving her grandfather a tour of their new home. Her grandfather noticed several bookshelves filled with Torah books, and upon learning of the couple's regular Torah study schedule, inquired incredulously, "So then when do you graduate?!"*

---

18   Rabbi Samson Raphael Hirsch, *Horeb* (New York: The Soncino Press Ltd., 2002), p. 3.

The answer is, of course, never. Torah study is a lifelong pursuit:

- Men have an obligation to learn Torah and to develop mastery and scholarship in it to the capacity that they are capable of. His Torah will create the energy required to build a Jewish-centered life and worldview.
- Women's Torah learning inspires day-to-day living and creates a connection to Hashem and the Jewish people. Her Torah will deepen and strengthen the values she seeks to cultivate within herself and also those she strives to imbue in the next generation of committed Jews.

Constructive Frustration

Baalei teshuvah are often frustrated and overwhelmed by having to catch up on many years' worth of Torah-learning skills and knowledge. Yet motivation and desire are often the bedrock of true accomplishment and all efforts toward greatness. It is well-known that Rabbi Akiva began learning Torah at age forty, attending school classes with children until, eventually, not only was he counted among the generation's greatest Torah scholars but he became their teacher as well. The frustration felt can be channeled into fuel for hard work, dedication, and, eventually, accomplishment.

In her class on Miriam HaNeviah, Rebbetzin Tzipporah Heller asks a logical question. When the Jews left Egypt, the Torah says that Miriam took out her tambourine and led the women in song to praise and thank Hashem. A tambourine is an unusual packing item when one is leaving the treacherous reality of slavery! When did she think to take that tambourine? And why?

Rebbetzin Heller explains that Miriam lived in the darkest time in Jewish history. And as her name itself reveals, she saw and experienced the bitterness of Egyptian slavery, as "Miriam" contains the word "*mar*," meaning "bitter." And yet, she had *emunah* that Hashem would rescue the Jewish people, that He would free them to be able to live a life that was true to their Jewish heritage and identity. Bringing along a tambourine to celebrate the first moments of that freedom was as much a part of her reality as the bitterness that surrounded her. To be bitter is a different state than depression. Depression is the inability to engage in and be responsive to the demands, challenges, and joys of life. Bitterness, on the other hand, is like the experience of putting salt into one's coffee instead of sugar as intended. It is a proactive response to challenge and even suffering. Bitterness combined with *emunah* results in redemption. Being in touch with reality but always recognizing God's hand in it propels one to succeed and triumph over the inevitable struggles that life presents.

In this way, the *baal teshuvah*'s frustration in having to "make up" on skills and knowledge can be productive. Perhaps the bitterness can give way to a strengthened effort, to an inspired and focused drive to attain. The person who espouses this attitude will not only rapidly catch up in terms of overall Torah knowledge, they will often surpass their counterparts because the knowledge they gain will be deeper and more integrated. It will be the fruit of hard work and dedication and it will be positively impacted by maturity and life experience. They will "own it" and understand it in a more sophisticated way than the person who first learned that piece of Torah as an elementary school student and never went beyond that level of understanding.

A man in his mid-thirties spent his first decade of observant life dedicating early-morning and late-night hours to catching up on fundamental Jewish knowledge and the building blocks of textual Torah study. Now, with some flexibility in his career, he is able to increase the time allotted to his Torah learning. As he joins an afternoon kollel program, he finds that he is on par with young men who have been studying at advanced levels for many years. His satisfaction is great and well-earned.

On a Practical Level

A person should begin his personal Torah-learning enrichment program with whatever interests him and feels within reach, given his schedule, time availability, and current level of learning. Success breeds further success, so it is best to begin with the type and subject of learning to which one feels a connection and of which one can make a personal acquisition, rather than what may appear more prestigious or on a higher level.

It is also important to keep in mind the principle that one must learn to walk before they can run. Learning is a lifelong process. While one may feel particularly drawn to certain advanced areas of Torah study, they may better facilitate their long-term growth and success in Torah and Judaism by beginning with the basics, such as translation of the siddur, the Rabbinic Hebrew language and grammar used in books of Jewish law, and the significant figures throughout Tanach.

> *In an extreme example, a young man with minimal Jewish education arrived at yeshiva in Eretz Yisrael, inspired to broaden and deepen his Torah knowledge and connection. But upon sitting in his first few classes in Chumash, Introduction to Talmud Study, and Jewish philosophy, he felt that his time would be better spent in his dorm room, studying Kabbalah.*

He was seeking something spiritual but didn't have enough patience to acquire the right keys to access it.

In a much more common example:

> *A young woman, who had been attending Torah classes for years, met with her weekly study partner to learn about Passover. She was able to recite all the deep philosophical points on freedom and the timeless messages for rebirth and renewal that the holiday of Passover holds, but could not place Miriam or her relevance and contribution to the events of the story. While quite familiar with complex ideas and lessons, the basic details of the Jewish experience in Egypt and its place within Jewish history was blurry in her mind.*

The point is that the more one is familiar with the foundational building blocks of Torah, the deeper their connection with their learning will be, enabling them to not only learn more in the future, but also to truly understand and benefit from that learning.

Never Give Up

The Talmud says: "In the way that a person wishes to go, so Heaven will lead him."[19] The level of foundational Jewish knowledge at which one begins is out of his control. The place where one's Torah-learning journey takes him or her directly correlates with one's aspirations, goals, and vision. Many *baalei teshuvah* who are accomplished in their careers and personal endeavors sell themselves short in their quest to learn and acquire Torah. Torah learning and application of this knowledge will form the basis of the values and identity of both individuals and families, and ultimately define the strength of their connection to Judaism. If there is anywhere to pour in effort, this is it. Just like physical muscle is built in the moments of physical exertion against resistance, so too frustration in this area should be perceived as the challenging yet constructive force against which we exert the necessary effort to build our Torah lenses and Jewish identities.

19   *Makkos* 10b.

Keeping
the Inspiration Alive

The beginning stages of marriage are often characterized by infatuation, with big, romantic overtures being a staple in the dynamic between spouses. Every new piece of information learned about one another and every new experience shared brings with it the excitement of novelty and potential. The infatuation phase is intense and effortless. That's because the couple senses the great possibilities that are inherent in their relationship but has not yet done the requisite work to turn them into reality. With the passage of time, as the relationship develops and the novelty wears off, it becomes clear that there are several defining characteristics which distinguish between couples:

- Some couples build a deeper, more mature love and connection that allows them to feel a sense of security and stability in their bond without as many public expressions or dramatic bids. They have realized much of their potential through their dedication and effort and can now enjoy the tangible return on this investment.

- Other couples, in contrast, will have relied so heavily and exclusively on the feelings and expressions of romance that when these diminish in frequency and intensity, they find that they haven't built the true foundation required for a long-lasting relationship. They are disappointed in the sense of lost love, when, in fact, they never began to create love in the first place.

This phase of romance and infatuation is not exclusive to love relationships. It is a common experience in the beginning phases of any new endeavor that holds potential for the one exploring or engaging in it. It can also be described as inspiration. The *Rambam*[20] gives the following analogy to understand the experience and boundaries of inspiration. Imagine walking down a dark street, trying to move ahead despite the diminished capacity to see where you are heading. Suddenly and momentarily, lightning strikes the path ahead, and for a brief moment the entire road becomes illuminated—your destination and the path leading to it suddenly become visible. It is a moment of great clarity, but just as soon as it comes, it's gone. As a result, it cannot support anything, nor can it serve as a foundation of any kind. If we wish to arrive at our destination, we must begin to walk along that path, equipped with that image of clarity and direction to guide us. The experience of momentary illumination is significant only insofar as it guides and inspires us to begin the journey. But until we begin to take steps toward our destination, that image is meaningless because we will not actually get any further than we are now. As inspired as we may have felt in the moment, in truth we have not yet moved at all. Only once the clarity departs, and the darkness once again sets in, can we truly begin walking, moving closer to our destination.

Rabbi Akiva Tatz[21] outlines three stages of inspiration:

- First there is an initial flash of inspiration, an undeserved gift that shows us the peak of what is possible.

---

20 Maimonides, *The Guide for the Perplexed* (La Vergne: BN Publishing, 2007), p. 3.
21 Rabbi Akiva Tatz, *Living Inspired* (Southfield: Targum, 1993), pp. 21–28.

- This is followed by a difficult period of trials and tribulations, during which we must work hard.
- This is followed by a final period of "transcendence," where we've fully earned and integrated the inspiration. To the extent that we have attained this level of transcendence, we no longer need to rely on the intensity and constancy of the initial inspiration in order to remain committed and satisfied with our overall endeavor.

Consider our medical student from the previous chapter attending an open house. Imagine the sense of inspiration he or she feels upon learning the benefits and potential outcomes of the medical school program. It is exciting, and ultimate success appears easily achievable, so long as the journey toward becoming a doctor has not yet begun. Yet despite the years of hard work and focused effort required for success in medical school, combined with the dedication needed to become an outstanding doctor, it is likely that the development of expertise, the impact made on the lives of countless patients, and the feeling of making a valuable contribution to society will make all that hard work seem worthwhile. This, in turn, provides deep motivation to continue and persist in the effort.

Stages of Growth

The beginning stages of Jewish growth and development are fueled by the inspiration of truth and a vision of the path toward fulfillment and happiness in life. Every Torah class and Shabbos meal feels like a new window, opening to beautiful, breathtaking scenery. Each new mitzvah taken upon oneself feels like an exhilarating climb to a gorgeous mountain top. But when it becomes ours, when we have reached the first, or perhaps the first few, major peaks in the mountain, when we not only gaze through the window at the beautiful view but also go out there and set up camp, life can feel mundane and ordinary. We may feel a lack in the intensity and excitement that encouraged us as we threw ourselves into Jewish life at the outset.

At some point we have "arrived," and the growth becomes incremental. It's not changing our lives rapidly with each mitzvah that's taken on. Rather, the growth may be externally smaller but should be internally deeper. We see this in the development of a human being. Within the first year of life a child changes in more developmentally significant ways than in any subsequent year of life. However, we understand that while the growth continues, it may not be as perceptible—but it is equally important to the overall development of the person. In many ways, it is less obvious but more mature. It is gradual and takes place deeper, below the surface. We should not be discouraged by this fact. Rather, we should understand that it is natural and a positive indicator that our growth is healthy, steady, and mature.

Reexamining Our Starting Point

This is an opportune time to consider what it is that brought us here to begin with. How can we take that as a starting point and reacquire Torah in a deeper, more sophisticated way? Was our initial motivation an understanding and discovery of truth, an unfulfilled need, an emotional connection to the Jewish community?

Judaism alone will not fix emotional (or other) problems, nor will it ensure a close, warm family, happiness, or anything else. Rather, the Torah contains the set of tools that, if used properly, can help one acquire happiness and success in life. Our emotional well-being and living of a Torah life are two separate tasks, with one serving in many ways as a prerequisite for the other.

It is not uncommon to find individuals who are frustrated in their Jewish lives, but the roots of this frustration are unrelated to Judaism. Being honest with oneself is critical in identifying the causes of one's dissatisfaction, and ultimately the best way to address these. For example, a truly philosophical question related to the role of women in Judaism can be examined through classes, conversations with knowledgeable teachers, or reading about the topic. Conversely, a woman who is experiencing difficulty in her marriage and complains about how unfair it feels to have her husband leave frequently for learning or davening will benefit from working through her relationship challenges before exploring the difference in expectations for men and women in *frum* society.

Our emotional well-being, our character, stability, and mental health can be likened to a cup, and Torah to the water that is poured in to quench one's thirst. If the cup has holes, the water will fall right through regardless of the amount that is poured in. A cup with a complete or mended surface will be able to hold water poured in, and with enough water can even spill over and provide nourishment outside of itself.

Inspiration over Time

We should not assume that once we become observant we no longer need inspiration. Instead, we need to proactively seek it out and create it for ourselves. Whether it is a *shiur*, a particular *chessed* project, or a trip into nature, we can—and should—engage in experiences that rejuvenate our Jewish life and connection with Hashem. Surrounding ourselves with other individuals who are also growth-oriented and living meaningful Jewish lives will also go a long way to creating the supportive and nurturing environment we need. While the explosive epiphanies of clarity we experienced in the initial stages may become increasingly few and far between as time goes on, our ongoing efforts to connect with positive individuals and invigorate ourselves with up-lifting experiences will enable us to keep climbing. In doing so, we will reach even higher peaks and witness even more spectacular views. We will take ownership over our own inspiration and tune in to the smaller and quieter moments, when Hashem opens a doorway for us to connect and reconnect with Him.

> I was once teaching a kallah, and on a particular day she stayed after our session.
>
> "Is it strange that I feel so strongly that he is my soulmate?" she asked, referring to her fiancé. "No," I told her. "It's not strange. Still, this feeling alone, as intense as it may be right now, will not sustain or guarantee a successful marriage."
>
> Unfortunately, this couple got divorced only a few short years later. The feeling was there, but the necessary steps to creating a dynamic and lasting relationship were not taken.

In other words, inspiration that is concretized into daily living endures and creates possibilities for further inspiration. Inspiration that is relied on as the basis of our lives cannot produce the desired result. Ultimately, we need to know that we are here to do *retzon Hashem* regardless of how it feels at any given moment. True and lasting happiness comes from pursuing the right thing, as opposed to engaging in experiences that just feel good. A person with the right mindset will find inspiration but will not become dependent on its frequency or intensity to reinforce his life decisions.

We cannot forget that the very path—and the great potential that lay ahead of it—that we saw for ourselves during those initial flash-of-lighting moments at the beginning of our journey is mitzvah observance itself. It is not coincidental that the word "halachah" comes from the root "*holech*—to walk." Adherence to and growth within the framework of halachah creates the path that we forge toward our greatest selves. The more we are cognizant of this, the more the walk itself will provide renewed inspiration and propel us ahead.

Confronting
the FFB World

F requently, *baalei teshuvah* find that the experiences they have once they are members of the *frum* community do not match up with the picture they had developed as visitors.

As we embark on our journey, we often feel that we are signing up to live among inspired, growth-oriented people like ourselves. We assume that we are entering a system where families and individuals uphold the values that are instilled through mitzvah observance and therefore lead happier, more successful lives than those on the outside. And what we find can be disappointing. Yes, there will certainly be people who live as we hoped—but they may be the select few. More commonly, we will encounter regular people, with regular struggles, for whom happiness and inspiration can be elusive, and life just as hectic, stressful, and often mundane as it is everywhere. Furthermore, we begin to notice shortcomings, such as individuals who struggle with the fundamentals of *emunah*, basic mitzvah observance, *shalom bayis*, and effective parenting. Much to our dismay, we find systemic issues that pervade the educational and social institutions that we fought so hard to be a part of. People are suddenly not quite as warm as we remembered them to be. Some are more materialistic and superficial than we initially experienced or expected.

Perspective is everything. Our initial experiences were with individuals and families who were the cream of the crop. They were inspired and found meaning in their connection to Torah and mitzvos to the degree that it not only impacted them personally, but they even felt motivated to draw from their deep reservoirs to share with their fellow Jewish brothers and sisters. These people were warm, welcoming, and nonjudgmental. They were deep thinkers who, in their own quest, achieved the answers they needed to build the foundations of a Jewish life.

The Torah lifestyle and environment to which we were introduced as fresh BTs is in many ways not representative of the Jewish world at large. While this can be frustrating at first, there is great potential for deeper and more mature Jewish development if we utilize these experiences properly. We must acknowledge that the "FFB" (*frum*-from-birth) world is imperfect. *Yeridas ha'doros*, our global spiritual decline as a nation over the course of history, has taken a huge toll on the religious world. "*Frumkeit*"—outer expressions of religious devotion, which unfortunately many times are only external and ring hollow because their internal reality is missing, is one aspect of this *yeridas ha'doros*. The FFB world can at times appear to overemphasize *frumkeit* and other types of superficiality. It can also sometimes appear "cold" or unwelcoming. The voids, issues, and imperfections we perceive are real. Perhaps they are there because we have not yet dedicated ourselves to filling them, thereby becoming part of an eventual solution to the problems. The Jewish world is waiting for our much-needed contributions, and is negatively impacted when we fail to step up to the plate.

On an even more fundamental level, it is important that *baalei teshuvah* are able to feel comfortable and function positively within the larger observant community, which almost always means within FFB circles. We don't have to find our best friends here or pretend to relate in ways we simply don't; it's natural to connect most with people with whom you have the most in common. On the other hand, identifying with the larger community in which we find ourselves is vital to our ability to lead a successful spiritual life there. A community provides a sense of identity, support in times of need, and a sense of belonging to a larger reality and mission that extends beyond that of the individual. Our ability to navigate the social, spiritual, and educational constructs of the broader community in many ways impacts the degree of success reached in our personal spiritual journey as well. It is no coincidence that Judaism places a major emphasis on community, since the implications of halachah are such that an ideal Torah life exists within communal life. In *Pirkei Avos*, we are told that "the world stands on three things: Torah, *avodah* (prayer), and *gemilus chassadim* (acts of kindness)."[22] Each of these categories is actualized through community life, and we can only truly fulfill the objectives of each within the structure of community.

A Myriad of Options

An important point to consider is whether your particular community is the best fit for you and your (future) spouse/children to settle in a permanent way. There are numerous observant communities all over the world, each with their distinct flavor and tone. Each community will have its own culture and set of norms, often reflecting to some degree the culture of the broader society and area amid which this community is located:

- Some are more homogenous, while others reflect a broad spectrum of *hashkafos* and personal backgrounds.
- Some are large with many shuls and schools to choose from. These communities can often feel less personal. Within them it is somewhat more difficult to form close connections to others. When there are so many people within each mini-group or microcommunity, people feel less of a need to initiate relationships with new or unfamiliar members.
- Other communities are smaller and more cohesive. Here, it is commonly easier to meet and connect to others, but options for types of schools and shuls are naturally more limited.

---

22   *Pirkei Avos* 1:2.

- Some communities will prove to be easier than others for *baalei teshuvah* to integrate into and become respected, appreciated members within.

Due to family considerations, financial realities, and other factors, it is not always an option for individuals or families to relocate. However, if at all possible, it behooves individuals and families to consider living in a community that would best provide what they need to thrive as healthy, happily committed Torah Jews.

Successful Navigation

Regardless of the specific community in which we live, the need to confront the FFB world remains. We may be "BTs" but our children will be "FFBs." In order to properly nourish their spiritual development, it is necessary to understand the realities in which they are growing up. The more we are able to navigate these challenges successfully ourselves, the more we are able to serve as positive and reliable guides for our children. If we want our kids to be well-adjusted, we must have the ability to adjust to our surroundings as well. It doesn't mean we have to be chameleons and sacrifice our individuality for the sake of "fitting in," nor does it mean we have to adopt practices and mentalities that are inherently detrimental to our spiritual growth. It simply means we must make an effort to bridge the gap between ideal and normal.

While there are certainly shortcomings in the FFB world, there are many beautiful things about it as well—and much to gain. The FFB world has a connection to *mesorah*—to the chain of Jewish life throughout the generations. *Mesorah* informs not only the halachic and Torah study process but also lends a sense of "normalcy" within Torah living. Since the Torah is a living organism, its adaptation throughout history and across societies can only be learned in real time, through the experience of life with others who are committed to it and have learned from their parents and grandparents what that commitment looks like on a practical level.

Often, in their passion and zeal, *baalei teshuvah* have extremely high expectations of themselves and others. Sometimes these expectations are unrealistic. If we expect too much, we set ourselves and our children up for spiritual disappointment and ultimately failure:

- Do we pressure or punish a three-year-old who doesn't feel like washing *netilas yadayim*?
- Do we become flabbergasted when we see *yeshiva bachurim* who beg their parents to buy them brand-name socks, striking us as more materialistic than we would hope for in a budding Torah scholar?

Perhaps some exposure to the FFB world will broaden our perspective. Perhaps it will make us realize that a happy three-year-old, and not an overly pressurized one, will be more likely to become an older child, teenager, and adult for whom *netilas yadayim* is a given. And when we recall the interests of the teenagers we grew up with, all of a sudden brand-name socks seem like a very desirable outlet.

In addition to gaining healthier expectations for our *frum* lives, the FFB world gifts its members insight into what true *chessed* and community look like. In the secular world, the concept of communal life is virtually nonexistent. People rarely know their neighbors' names, much less interact with them in meaningful ways. The idea that families will regularly host both friends and strangers in their homes to share in joyful occasions as well as in times of need is unheard of in the world at large. The number of *chessed* organizations and *gemachim* in established communities reflects the incredible support available for virtually every life stage and need. Often, those who live as part of *frum* communities are so accustomed to these aspects of communal life that they forget how rare they truly are.

> *A woman who worked in an office environment was talking to a coworker about a friend who recently had a baby. When this non-Jewish coworker heard about the weeks' worth of meals that friends, neighbors, and synagogue acquaintances signed up to deliver to this woman, along with the free cleaning help that was arranged by a local organization, she was beside herself. "It's really incredible what you guys have. You know, a real*

*sense of community, people who know you and are there for
you. I live in a large high-rise in the city. Even though the building has hundreds of units, I don't know anyone. I walk through
busy streets and ride on a packed subway on my commute to
work, and yet I'm all alone. What you have is so special, I ad-
mire it so much." These thoughts made the observant woman
pause. She had taken these unique aspects of her community
for granted. This interaction reminded her how truly remarkable the Jewish community is.*

We can acknowledge that the FFB world is far from perfect while
simultaneously learning from it in beneficial ways and appreciating all
the gifts it has to offer.

The Root of the Behavior

Attempting to understand why certain things are the norm in the
FFB world and then deciding whether or not we will integrate them into
our homes and families will aid our ability to successfully navigate it.
We need to distinguish whether any particular norm stems from a true
Torah concept or is irrelevant to Torah and has simply become a cultural
standard. We can do the above by distinguishing between the following
possibilities in a given situation where we try to understand the behavior we see. We need to ask ourselves: is what I'm seeing halachah,
minhag, chumrah, sensitivity, culture, or shortcoming:

- **Halachah** is Jewish law, whether it is of *d'Oraisa* (Biblical) or
  d'Rabbanan (Rabbinic) origin. Starting a fire and moving money
  on Shabbos are both halachically prohibited.
- *Minhag* is a custom that became widespread within Jewish
  society over the course of time and is therefore treated with
  reverence. Wearing a *kippah* for men, and a bride and groom
  not having contact with one another for the week leading up
  to their wedding are both widespread *minhagim* among most
  Jewish communities.
- *Chumrah* is a stringency in a certain area of Jewish law. A *chumrah*
  must be rooted in the halachic discussions of the Oral Law. For

women, wearing stockings in addition to a skirt that covers the knees, in order to have some type of covering from the knee to the ankle, is a *chumrah*. This is a very accepted *chumrah* in certain communities and is considered *"minhag ha'makom"* there—the standard practice in that place or among that group of people.

- **Sensitivities** are much more broad and can exist on a communal or personal level. A sensitivity takes into account the spirit, not only the letter, of the law. For example, in some communities, husbands and wives generally refrain from public touching of any kind in an effort to maintain a heightened sense of modesty around their relationship.

- **Culture** exists within any society, group of people, or institution. Culture represents the norms and expectations of a group that formed organically, with or without connection to the underlying philosophies of that group. Individual universities have unique cultures that reflect the demographics and focus of that particular institution. Some are known to be more about socializing than studying, others more focused on practical trade, while others carry an elitist tone. And academia as a whole tends to have a generally progressive, liberal culture to it as well. Families have cultures. Some families are more formal and others more casual. The culture of a family will inform expectations surrounding the style, nature, and frequency of family communication, get-togethers, overall involvement, and much more. The FFB world is no exception. A *chassan* purchasing a large floral centerpiece for a *vort*, newlyweds joining parents for Shabbos meals on a weekly basis and for *Yamim Tovim* for years, and certain styles of dress—whether European-style Shabbos clothing for children or all-black outfits for women—are all examples of the norms that are part of *"frum* culture." These are not necessarily linked to Torah ideals, and other than understanding them for what they are, there is no inherent value in mimicking these in our own lives unless we feel drawn to do so.

- Just as culture exists among all groups, **shortcomings** do as well. Shortcomings are a natural part of all human life. The girls in seminary who cry themselves to sleep after being berated by mothers and sisters who are concerned that they will never get married due to the two pounds they gained that week are unfortunate. The obvious discrepancies between the handbook of a school and its students dress, behavior, and attitudes can be discouraging. The individuals and families who have different standards for behavior when on vacation versus when within the confines of their community blocks can be bewildering. The ability to recognize a shortcoming when it exists is the first step to making sure we are role models of more ideal behavior. Perhaps even more importantly, a more realistic view can also be a catalyst for increased kindness and compassion as we encounter and live with fellow Jews who are each on their own journey and level, often with good reason to be where they are when we take into account the totality of their own Jewish experience.

Just as in our relationships with secular family and friends, our interactions with people of different backgrounds within a Torah community will be greatly enhanced by a deep sense of confidence in our own behaviors as well as an understanding of theirs. This is because if we know the roots of what we see in our communities, we will be able to properly evaluate the experiences we have here, and there will be no need to feel insecure or defensive in response to behaviors or attitudes that differ from our own. We will also develop tools to mitigate the frustration we may experience at the shortcomings we notice. As it turns out, no one is spared from personal challenges, struggles, and mountains to climb. Internalizing the fact that FFBs are just normal people who happened to receive Torah and the tools for attaining greatness at birth and not later in life does not immunize them from challenges or imperfections. It simply sets them up for a different set of them.

Carrying Ourselves with Dignity

In order to be successful in our communities, we do not need to hide our backgrounds. We have a lot to be proud of and also a lot to contribute. At the same time, just like a person is not allowed to remind a BT about aspects of his background that might make him uncomfortable or demean him, so too it stands to reason that we should not be doing this to ourselves. We need to think carefully about which parts of our experiences from our secular lives we want to share with others. Which aspects of our family dynamics or challenges that we went through in becoming *frum* would reflect positively on the person we have grown to become, and which would be a negation of that same person? We cannot naively think that every person we encounter is there to cheer us on in life. Other's negative reactions to our unfiltered sharing is not a poor reflection of their *middos* but rather of our lack of judgment in carrying ourselves in ways that are dignified and self-respecting.

Sometimes we will receive positive reactions to sharing highly personal information with others, whether over a Shabbos meal or in passing. This is still not a good indicator that we should, in fact, be sharing these sensitive parts of our lives with others. Sharing details about our struggles in our relationship with our families, dating, or various struggles or "unkosher" experiences from our past, among other things, in an indiscriminate way may feed someone's innocent curiosity but will negatively impact our own sense of self and impede our standing as an equal member of the community we seek to be a part of. As a student once exclaimed in frustration, "If one more random person asks about the details of my dating, I'm going to start asking them how their marriage is going!"

We need to form a strong personal support system within the broader community, and as a result, we will be informed, generally positive members of this larger whole. In this state we will be able to successfully navigate both the highs and the lows of an immersive Jewish life. And we will serve as great guides for our children, who will depend on our sense of security and well-being to begin building their own.

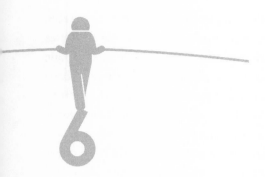

True
Greatness

In order to grow and thrive spiritually, it's essential for us to learn to balance two important ideals: striving for greatness, while simultaneously retaining a focus on normalcy, i.e., being able to grow toward our potential while remaining grounded and connected to the world around us. In order to most effectively maintain long-term growth as healthy, balanced individuals, we need to carefully analyze both of these ideals and how they might be challenged in the times in which we live.

A Culture of Mediocrity

A number of recent national statistics[23] have shown a sharp decline in several behaviors among teenagers over the course of two decades, which were seen as staples of the adolescent experience only a short time ago. Experiences such as spending the majority of their free

---

23   https://www.theatlantic.com/magazine/archive/2017/09/has-the-smartphone-destroyed-a-generation/534198/

time with friends, dating, and even acquiring a driver's license, once the hallmarks of the adolescent fight for increased independence, are all on the decline. When exploring the factors presumed to have contributed to this trend, a startling and perhaps frightening picture emerges. These statistics correlate to the rise of social media: it seems that with so many hours spent staring at a screen and connecting to the world through a virtual medium, kids have lost the energy and drive to leave their houses and spend time together in person. Their desire for autonomy has faded into a dependence on their parents and gadgets. These trends are a reflection on the society we live in. Loss of excitement, enthusiasm, and natural drives, even for less-than-ideal experiences and motives, is a net negative for individuals and society as a whole. This prevailing sense of complacency is what allows people to be satisfied with a mediocre status quo, both in relation to themselves and the world around then. Between experiences provided by advanced technologies and an overall state of comfort in which we live, we, as a society, have developed an apathy toward the acquisition of knowledge, true self-growth, and self-actualization.

Our inner drives motivate us, energize us, and enliven us. We can control and direct these for good or allow them to dominate and steer us toward physically and spiritually destructive ends. When we engage our energies, those that push and move us, we have a chance to do great things and, in the process, elevate ourselves as people. But when there is no drive, when all that exists is a superficial obedience, we cut ourselves off from true growth and from a real chance at accomplishing and creating in this world. We remain at peace with our mediocrity because we have lost the vision and the energy we need to build the best version of ourselves and our lives. In the end, we fail to truly live.

The Gemara relates[24] an astonishing account of Chazal davening to remove the inclination for idol worship from the Jewish people. When their prayers succeeded, they realized the power they wielded

---

24   *Yoma* 69b.

and proceeded to consider the removal of the inclination for immoral relations as well. However, when they did so, animals suddenly ceased to procreate, and all existence was threatened. Ultimately, they were forced to retract and allow this inclination to be reinstated. Incredibly, the same force that brings immorality into the world is the very element responsible for the existence of the world as well. Hashem gave us an evil inclination in order to struggle with it. The moment we cease struggling is also the moment we cease to be engaged, essentially alive members of His world.

Are We Immune?

It may seem that *baalei teshuvah* would be immune to this phenomenon given that they exuded much focus, energy, and passion to change their lives in pursuit of truth. But since *frum* life is not immune to the outside world and all its trends, we find a prevalence of apathy within the broader *frum* community as well. Stuck between the struggle for a secure sense of self on the one hand, and their attempts to fit in with their new surroundings on the other, BTs are also at risk for developing a certain sense of complacency and acceptance of mediocrity once they settle into their observant lives.

Hashem does not expect perfection. The Torah itself records the mistakes and flaws of our great leaders throughout Tanach. But one thing that we do not see is a lack of drive or motivation, a complacency that breeds apathy and mediocrity. All the great people throughout Jewish history felt they were part of a much larger story and mission than the mundane details and circumstances of their lives. This is true for each and every Jewish person. We are all here to do something in the world that is a reflection of our innate abilities, to harness our unique passions and energies, and direct them toward something purposeful that will benefit the world.

Amalek, the nation that represents the root of evil in the world and which we are commanded to uproot in order to bring the world to a state of perfection, attacked the Jewish people immediately upon their exit from slavery at the hands of the Egyptians. In describing the attack, the Torah uses the phrase "*asher korcha ba'derech*—they happened upon you along the way."[25] The Midrash,[26] in an alternative translation of the word "*korcha*" as "cooled you off," likens the attack to one who jumped into a scalding-hot bath. Although guaranteed to get burned, he was willing to accept the pain in order to accomplish his goal of cooling off the bath.

The nation of Amalek, characterized by their dedication, at any cost, to reduce and ultimately extinguish the flames of Jewish passion and energy for Torah and mitzvos, are the very antithesis of our mission in the world. Despite their dedication to fight against us in our goal of increasing spirituality in the world, they are only able to rise up when the Jewish people manifest a certain weakening in their own passion for carrying out their mission. The Midrash explains the significance of the location in which Amalek staged their attack. The verse says, "Amalek came and battled Israel in Rephidim."[27] The word "Rephidim" is interpreted by the Midrash[28] as an allusion to the words "*Rafu yedeihem*"—their hands weakened from their dedication to Torah. Likewise, we learn in *Megillas Esther* how it was a general laxity[29] on the part of the Jews that enabled Haman, scion of the Amalekite nation, to ascend to power and promulgate a decree to annihilate all the Jews. Before the Jews were able to supplant the decree and defeat their enemies, they had to rekindle the flames of Jewish observance and unity; only then could they emerge victorious. The two great Jews who led the nation at that time, Esther and Mordechai, characterize taking initiative, applying themselves with conviction and a sense of purpose to do what was necessary.

The entire concept of freedom versus slavery is encapsulated in the name Mitzrayim, which symbolizes the epitome of enslavement. The root of the experience of a Mitzrayim is "*meitzar*—constriction." Whether externally or internally imposed, a sense of limitation is the beginning of a diminished drive, which breeds spiritual atrophy. When there is no possibility for growth, deterioration and ultimate death are the natural and inevitable consequences.

---

25   *Devarim* 25:18.
26   *Midrash Tanchuma* 9.
27   *Shemos* 17:8.
28   *Mechilta*, ibid.
29   *Megillah* 12a.

In contrast, having a sense of context and a "big picture" perspective frees a person from the mundane and normal challenges of everyday life. Dreaming big opens pathways for growth and greatness. This is not about over-assessing our capabilities and what we expect from ourselves and others. Rather, it's about not selling ourselves short and just being average, or just doing the bare minimum required.

> *My husband and I attended parent-teacher conferences a number of years ago. Our daughter's teacher enthusiastically relayed that she was "doing great at the bottom of the average reading group" in her class. She may have been surprised to not see smiling faces reflecting her own. While all parents are biased, we sincerely felt that we had a good sense of our daughter's skills and abilities and that this was not an accurate reflection of her capabilities or potential. We left wondering if our society is one that is too quick to accept average performance without even attempting to see if there is more potential to explore or abilities to tap into.*

This mentality translates into an outlook on our spiritual lives as well. You can live by all the rules, that's good, Hashem wants that, but it's the bare minimum. Within the rules, Hashem wants you to be passionate, to have drive, take an interest in things, and bring your best self to the experience. In our very positive effort to not create a society that pushes or pressures too much, have we created one where not only are there few overachievers, there is very little motivation to achieve something great at all? Are people living by the rules, so to speak, but not seeing themselves and the light they are meant to shine from within? And given all the pressures and stressors of modern-day life, have we become too constrained and burdened to truly live and strive to be enthusiastic participants, with a great purpose, in the cosmic experience of Torah life and Jewish history?

There is a well-known anecdote of a truck driver who, in his work, frequently received speeding tickets. One time he was dispatched for a cross-country delivery by his manager, who was sure to send him off with stern warnings not to get any tickets. Upon returning, the driver proudly exclaimed, "This time, I did not get even one ticket!" When the manager gazed into the back of the truck, he was quite dismayed. "Perhaps you didn't get any tickets," he shouted, "but you haven't delivered the goods!" The "goods" are our personalities, abilities, energies, and passions. In our quest to "do everything right," we can't compromise the mission itself; we must "deliver the goods."

In truth, a sense of drive and passion to achieve greatness will impact every area of our lives and all the points discussed in this book. It will impact our sense of self, making it deeper and stronger. It will motivate us to apply ourselves, to seek out in all situations the opportunities to find ourselves and contribute to the people around us and to the *frum* society of which we are important members. In marriage, we will be two vibrant, generative individuals who connect to each other and to a shared mission. Beyond all the technicalities of life, it will be exciting to live with a person of vision and drive. And certainly, as part of parenting, we will give our children much more than a lap to sit on, hands to help them get dressed, and a watchful eye as they climb the jungle gym at the park. Our own sense of purpose and enthusiasm will become part of their vision and their own sense of identity. The technical parts of parenting, and of life, can feel overwhelming. However, we can rise above it and free ourselves from constriction to connect with something much bigger. This will provide much-needed energy and nourishment to all the areas of our life. Instead of merely existing, we can begin to truly live.

In *Mishlei* we read, "A refining pot is for silver, and the furnace for gold, and a man according to his praise."[30] While we typically understand this to mean that the way people praise a person characterizes him, Rabbeinu Yonah explains the phrase "a man according to his praise" to mean that a person is ultimately defined by those things that he or she praises. The things we get excited about, becoming animated and passionate as we discuss them, these are the true reflections of who we are as people. They drive our focus and activity and come to define

30   *Mishlei* 27:21.

who we are as people. We have to make sure there still remain areas in our lives that so deeply move us, and that this movement is one that brings us to our inherent, great potential.

The Great Balancing Act

While continuing to strive for greatness and expression of our spiritual potential, we must be aware of a crucial counterpoint to this idea. In a surprising statement, Shlomo HaMelech tells us in *Koheles*,[31] "*Al tehi tzaddik harbeh v'al tischakam yoser*," meaning that we shouldn't be too much of a *tzaddik*! Nor should we be too wise.

This seems shocking! Striving for *chochmah* and righteousness seems to be the basis of Torah life!

Shlomo HaMelech is imparting an important truth. We should strive to be great, to be holy, but not greater and holier than all others. The *mefarshim* on this *pasuk*[32] caution—if we are too holy, no one will want to be around us and we will remain isolated. Others include that this *pasuk* is a reference to Shaul HaMelech, who, in his attempt to act compassionately, enabled the greatest enemy of the Jewish people to be perpetuated. Hashem knows what He is doing. If He told us to do or not do something, we don't have to worry too much about exerting ourselves to be more *frum* than Hashem Himself intended.

This implies that we need to master the careful balance between being real and authentic but also never settling and always striving for greatness. We have to find a balance between not being complacent and stagnant in our growth on one hand, or overly pressuring and intense on the other. It is important to recognize the inherent greatness that exists in being normal. Torah and its implications for character and lifestyle should more or less define my "norm." This might mean that a certain standard within my *frum* community may actually be beneath what I would consider "normal" for myself. We do not need to limit ourselves to mediocrity but rather push ourselves toward personal greatness in a healthy way.

---

31   *Koheles* 7:16.
32   *Metzudas David*, ibid.

Why Is This Hard for Us?

Oftentimes, it is the ability to deviate from society's expectations and resist conforming that allowed a *baal teshuvah* to pursue truth and an alternate lifestyle to what they grew up with. It is these very same qualities that will need to be carefully directed once they have settled into the observant life they pursued with the initial excitement of forging ahead on an as-yet-uncleared path.

Once we have arrived at the conclusion that Torah and mitzvah observance are the foundations for the life we will live, it behooves us to become aware of our new landscape and realize that while our free and critical thinking will benefit us wherever we go, we need to check it against the truth we have arrived at so painstakingly. By making sure we can generally see ourselves as a part of a larger community, with its set of norms and standards, we can ensure our connection to *mesorah*. In a sense, we must strive to master the art of fitting in without losing ourselves in the process. An individual who is successful in this endeavor will be both a positive member of his or her community and a true contributor to its positive spiritual and social development as well.

Going Above and Beyond

"Taking on" a specific behavior or standard that goes beyond the basic standards of halachah that one's community has established should be considered carefully. Specifically, we should consider the root of the behavior as well as that of our desire to act in a way that is stricter or more elevated than the accepted norms of the surroundings we have chosen for ourselves.

Steps when considering a new behavior, practice, or custom:

1. **Identify the nature of the behavior**. Under what umbrella category does it fall? Is it a *chumrah*, sensitivity, or something else?
2. **Perform a cost-benefit analysis**. Will this create further strife or distance between myself and my family? Is that necessary or truly beneficial in my case? What do I gain, and does anyone around me lose out?
3. **Seek out the true nature of your intentions**. It is important to be honest with where you are "holding." Am I really at the level

where taking on this particular thing will be in line with where I'm at in other areas, a sincere effort in *avodas Hashem*? Or am I compensating for an insecurity?

4. **Ask yourslef if you are a true exception for whom this behavior is healthy and real.** Am I trying to send my husband out to learn for twenty-four years because Rachel, the wife of Rabbi Akiva, did in the times of the Gemara? Have my words and language suddenly become accented by a Yiddish tone and flavor where one never existed all these years and decades?

A young woman, growing in her mitzvah observance, approached her mentor for feedback on her intended next Jewish steps. Since she had taken on wearing skirts about a month earlier, she was considering perhaps wearing tights and stockings regularly. Her mentor wisely suggested that perhaps she should learn how to daven and keep kosher in a more careful manner before taking on something that could result in more external validation but would be far less basic or fundamental than other areas of Torah observance.

More often than not, the louder and more external the behavior we are considering, the more suspicious we should be of it and question if it is truly the next healthy step in our growth in *avodas Hashem*.

When we hear inspiring stories about the great *tzaddikim* and *tzidkaniyos* of the Tanach, Gemara, and generations past, we must always process them through the filter of our current generation. It is correct and praiseworthy to feel inspired when we read about Kimchis,[33] who never uncovered her hair under any circumstances, or *gedolim* who learned for eighteen hours a day. We cannot and should not try to be like them in all ways or "go so far," but we can apply their lessons by taking on small but effective commitments in similar areas. In so doing,

---

33   *Yoma* 47a.

we are formulating a healthy, balanced approach that ensures that our inspiration persists, and will continue to impact ourselves and our children.

Greatness ultimately comes from creating a vision that we have cross-checked with *daas Torah* and those we have established as our role models in Torah living, and then setting realistic and attainable goals to reach that vision. It is imperative to strive for great spiritual heights while simultaneously remaining relatable and able to integrate into our broader Torah-true surroundings.

It's in the Small Things

The depth of one's greatness is often seen in the quieter, objectively smaller ways that a person impacts others and the world around him through the high levels that he himself has attained. Consider the following example:

> *A nine-year-old boy came home from school to find that his father's Rosh Yeshiva, a great Torah scholar, was visiting their home. He was in town as part of a fund-raising trip that took him all over the country in the span of just several days. His trip was packed from morning to night with meetings, and there was no doubt that his time and attention were in constant high demand. When the Rosh Yeshiva saw the boy, he asked him to share some words of Torah that he had learned in school. The boy shared a d'var Torah that he had recently learned. The Rosh Yeshiva sat back with a big smile and exclaimed, "That was beautiful. Wow, thank you for sharing that."*
>
> *Several days later, a letter came in the mail. It was an acceptance letter from this Rosh Yeshiva to his yeshiva, addressed to none other than this nine-year-old boy. In the letter, the Rosh Yeshiva wrote that when the time comes he would be looking forward to accepting this boy into his esteemed institution.*

A permanent mark was left on the life of this boy. For years he would recall the interaction, and the letter received from this *talmid chacham,* with excitement and joy. His eyes would light up every time someone mentioned yeshiva, and he would proudly mention that he already got his acceptance letter. No doubt, his eagerness and love of *limud haTorah* were increased exponentially. It was just a small, mostly unknown act. It took an extra ounce of sensitivity, of thought, amid objectively much more important items on the agenda. But it deeply impacted another person's life in a major way. The true greatness of even well-known individuals, whose accomplished stature is recognized, is often found in the quieter parts of their lives.

The depth of Hashem's greatness is hidden. So too, the greatness of His servants and representatives in this world is also found in the quiet but truly deep ways that a person builds himself up and then directs all that he has to influence the life of another. When we embark on paths toward greatness, it is worthwhile for us to consider not how to do more than Hashem and His Torah, but rather how we can truly emulate Hashem and His Torah.

Becoming
a Wellspring for Giving

The Gemara says[34] that the Jewish people are known for three things: They are known to be *rachmanim* (merciful), *bayshanim* (possessing shame), and *gomlei chassadim* (people who do acts of kindness for others). These character traits stand out as the defining features of our nation and the individuals who comprise it. In other words, a Jewish person is defined more by his ability to give and do for others than his ability to amass physical and even spiritual wealth in a purely self-focused and self-contained way.

A Shift in Thinking

Sometimes, it requires a mental shift for *baalei teshuvah* to place themselves on the giving versus receiving end. This is in no way because *baalei teshuvah* are selfish or greedy in essence. Rather, it often stems from the fact that *baalei teshuvah* have become accustomed to

---

34   *Yevamos* 79a.

receiving, especially in their initial interactions with Jewish individuals and the Jewish community. Think back to the initial experiences that exposed you to Judaism and all the way through the early phases of growth in mitzvah observance. Not only were there countless classes available on any Jewish topic of interest, families who welcomed you with open arms into their homes and to their Shabbos tables, heavily subsidized trips and overseas learning opportunities, but you were applauded and praised for taking advantage of any of these! *Baalei teshuvah* come to assume that it is the most natural thing for families to regularly host strangers in their homes and give of their time, energy, and emotional and financial resources to feed, teach, and support other Jews in any number of ways. And this couldn't be more true! This *should* be the natural reality for a Jewish person. However, some *baalei teshuvah* don't internalize that this means that they, too, are held to these expectations once they themselves enter the community as *frum* Jews.

> *I once took a group of kallahs on a mikveh tour prior to their weddings. As we learned about the facility and the amenities available to the women who use it to fulfill one of the most beautiful and fundamental mitzvos, I mentioned that there is a suggested donation that each woman pays, to the best of her ability, each time she uses the mikveh. Among the group, three kallahs were baalos teshuvah and two grew up observant. The three women who took on Torah observance later in life were shocked that there was a fee associated with a community facility. They must have forgotten that the cleaning service, hot water, and clean linen were not mahn falling from the sky and that no one was entitled to these. Each community member readily participates in making this mitzvah a positive and pleasant experience for the entire community.*

Especially those of us who have benefited from the true kindness and spiritual gifts of others should feel motivated to find opportunities to emulate these incredible traits and become givers ourselves. We should naturally establish ourselves as contributive members of our family unit, community, and the entire Jewish people.

Self-Sufficiency

Chazal speak at length[35] about how a person should go to all ends to avoid becoming needy and dependent on others. On one hand, everyone needs and will benefit from support and connection to friends and role models. On the other hand, it is healthy and constructive for each person to strive for self-sufficiency and an other-oriented mentality. Once a person is married and has their own home, unless there is an extreme need, it should be the exception rather than the rule for the couple to request an invitation for others to have them over for Shabbos meals. When *baalei teshuvah* tell me that it is very difficult to make Shabbos every week, I tell them I find it difficult to be on top of my laundry, keep my house clean, and make dinner every night. Would they find it acceptable if I posted on Facebook or one of my WhatsApp groups asking if anyone could come over to mop my floor or cook dinner for my family that evening? Once a person establishes their own home, they are essentially assuming responsibility for the members of that home and their needs. Shabbos is a regular part of the Jewish home, much like dinner and homework and laundry. If a person needs tips on how to make Shabbos in a manageable and pleasant way, this is a great opportunity to approach someone who seems successful with this and learn from their wisdom and example. The *Yamim Tovim* are a time that have, most unfortunately, become associated with stress in many homes, but *baalei teshuvah* in particular often feel short-changed during these times. Young couples will notice that their friends and neighbors seem to pack up and crash at their parents' homes, seemingly absolved of the work, stress, and financial burden of making Yom Tov at home. In some circles this can go on well past the couple's first decade of marriage.

A young woman, while growing in her Torah observance in her late teens, developed a close relationship with a warm

---

35   *Pesachim* 113a; *Pirkei Avos* 2:2; *Rabbeinu Yonah*, ibid.; *Mishlei* 5:15, 15:27 as explained by Rav Shlomo Wolbe, *zt"l*, in *Maamarei Hadrachah L'Chassanim* 2:1, p. 8.

and giving family in her community. She would spend most Shabbosim with this family, enjoying the warm atmosphere and gaining immensely through observing a Torah-true home in action. She spent several years this way, until she went to seminary. Once she returned from seminary, she resumed weekly attendance, and the family was happy to once again share their home and their Shabbos with her. Shortly after, she got married and (with her new husband) settled into her home and life within the community. Still, she asked to come on a weekly basis for Shabbos meals to this family. The couple's first child was already a toddler and they were still requesting to move in for each Yom Tov with this family! By this time, the host family had several married children who were also coming home for chagim and felt understandably burdened by the needs and expectations of this young woman whom they otherwise sincerely enjoyed and wanted to continue giving to in more manageable ways, while remaining involved in her life on an ongoing basis. There is, after all, a limit.

More often than not, those individuals and families who open their homes and hearts to their fellow Jewish brothers and sisters very much enjoy the opportunity to contribute and make a positive impact on someone's life. Becoming needy or dependent on others is often not to the detriment of the giver, regardless of the fact that they may feel some burden as a result. The real detriment is to the one who remains a taker, perpetually requiring large investments from others toward their basic functioning. They are the ones who miss the opportunity to grow themselves, becoming more capable, self-sufficient, and contributive.

Capitalizing on Our Situation

Instead of feeling frustrated or making excessive demands of others, *baalei teshuvah* can capitalize on this situation to form strengths and abilities their FFB counterparts do not have—and may even be envious of when the inevitable time comes for them to make Shabbos or Yom Tov on their own. While still young and having relatively fewer demands due to fewer children and overall lifestyle needs, *baalei teshuvah* can learn the ropes of making Yom Tov, even becoming quite skilled at it. One day, their FFB friends may come to them for advice on how to manage it all and they will have wisdom to share from their own experiences.

Everyone needs a break sometimes, or extra support during a particularly challenging week. If a couple has a close network of friends, a close mentor, or a family they can lean upon in times of need, it is, of course, acceptable and even necessary that they utilize these resources. But support and dependence are not one and the same. Support ultimately enhances our ability to function independently and optimally. In contrast, dependence atrophies our ability to do so.

Seeing Ourselves as Givers

Self-perception plays a key role in being a giver. Seeing ourselves in the position of a giver enables us to become one. Now we can teach someone, host guests in our home, and contribute our unique skills and talents to benefit those around us. We do not have to know everything there is to teach or have all the resources in the world to give. Once a person develops the mindset of a giver, they suddenly find a myriad of causes and voids, all awaiting their unique contribution. Take, for example, the single young woman who, while at a stage in her life where she relied on other's hospitality for Shabbos meals, would always arrive at her host's homes with candy for the kids, a big warm smile, and a helping hand throughout the meal. This might not seem extraordinary, but it is not as common as we might think. This woman utilized a situation where one is naturally a recipient of other's *chessed*, and within it, became a giver. Needless to say, she received a steady flow of eager invites for Shabbos and Yom Tov meals in her community. If our emotional and spiritual cup is overflowing, if we are leading productive and fulfilling Jewish lives, there is inevitably a multitude of ways to direct that overflow in an outward direction and use it to benefit others and the world around us.

Organized Chessed

We live in a time where there is an established organization or profession for almost every type of *chessed* imaginable:

- We have outreach organizations with *kiruv* professionals that span the globe.
- There are other organizations established to meet the needs of youth-at-risk within our communities.
- Professional *shadchanim* are available in every city with a Jewish community to facilitate new marriages.
- There are organizations dedicated to meeting the emotional and physical needs of families who are struggling with a sick child.
- Local *bikur cholim* organizations provide meals and other forms of support for families with a loved one in the hospital.

On one hand, this is an incredible phenomenon that reflects the Jewish desire to heal, repair, build, and improve the world. Countless individuals and families are positively impacted by the streamlined *chessed* operations that these initiatives provide. On the other hand, with so many organized activities and services, individuals may begin to feel that they are not needed as part of the effort. As more mitzvos continue to become filed for not-for-profit status on a regular basis, an individual Jew may begin to think that a professional designation is required for their fulfillment. In truth, every Jew has been mandated by God to feel, think, and behave as *"kol Yisrael areivim zeh la'zeh."*[36] The well-being and needs of every Jew, in addition to those of the community at large, are the responsibility of every single Jewish person. There is no one individual who can address every need. That is why the unique creativity, talents, and skills of a variety of people are desperately needed. A forty-hour-per-week job and a salary are not prerequisites to addressing a need, filling a void, and utilizing one's abilities to benefit others.

---

36   *Sanhedrin* 43b.

A young woman from a small out-of-town community, who had been dating for several years, decided to relocate to a city with a larger Jewish community in hopes that this would make it easier to meet people. Prior to moving, she reached out to several recently married friends. Since they themselves had gotten married only a short time earlier, their husbands certainly had many single friends. She thought perhaps they could brainstorm some potential date ideas for her in her new city. All of them kindly responded that she should speak to a shadchan when she arrives at her destination.

Unfortunately, these couples completely missed the point. And more importantly, they missed an enormous opportunity. Either they had all too soon forgotten the stress and worry that pervade the dating process, where any suggestions for dates or introductions are so deeply appreciated, or perhaps they failed to recognize the unique position they were in to help a friend in her search for her soulmate. They didn't realize that they had some "stake" in this mitzvah, that it wasn't someone else's exclusive domain.

A young couple, recently married and with a new baby, moved to a new community where they didn't know many people. The young woman began attending a shiur with other new wives and mothers and started to feel a sense of community with other like-minded women. Shortly after they settled in, this couple arranged to host a kiddush in honor of their daughter. All the women from the shiur were invited to join in the simchah. The teacher from the class also emphasized that this would be a great opportunity to show much-needed support and friendship during a challenging transition for this young family. While everyone theoretically agreed that this would be a great idea, on the actual day of the kiddush, there were barely any women from this class in attendance.

Everyone had legitimate excuses. Schedules are tight on Shabbos morning. Babies and toddlers need to be put down for their naps on time. And so on and so forth. But this is an oversight. Because Shabbos, their families, and their children would all ultimately benefit from the giving nature of their mother and wife. Giving that has been integrated into one's daily life and mentality need not be, and rarely consists of, life-altering actions. Rather, it is a meaningful as opposed to extensive or arduous investment of one's time, energy, resources, and focus.

Responsible Giving

Whenever we get involved in helping others, we have to be responsible givers. We need to avoid offering wisdom, tools, or resources that we ourselves do not have. A single woman cannot offer parenting advice to the mother of children spanning toddlerhood through adolescence. A *yeshiva bachur* cannot possibly give his married *chavrusa* insights into building a strong marriage. Our attempts at giving should not, in reality, be overtures that are compensating for deep insecurities or an unfulfilled sense of being needed. We have to know our limits and stay within our boundaries. But where we do possess ability, knowledge, and skill, we cannot miss out on the opportunity to direct those capabilities toward filling a need that Hashem has put right before us.

"The Work Is Not upon You to Finish..."

In *Parashas Pekudei*,[37] following the completion of the building of the *Mishkan*, *Rashi* explains that when the *Mishkan* was built, the workers could not erect it because of its massive weight. Hashem then told Moshe to erect it. The obvious question here is: If many people could not stand it up, how would it be possible for a single person to accomplish this task?

Rashi explains that when Hashem instructed Moshe to participate in the building of the Mishkan, He told Moshe to attempt to erect. And once Moshe would put in his effort, Hashem Himself would make it stand. Furthermore, Moshe would be credited with its standing.

Why? Why would Moshe be given credit for something he didn't actually do?

---

37   *Shemos* 39:33.

This seemingly minor episode in the Torah lends insight into one of the most important and fundamental principles in Jewish life. In reality, we are only able to perform any mitzvah because Hashem enables us to do so. Without *siyata d'Shmaya*, Heavenly assistance, we would not be able to accomplish anything, including the things that appear to be very much within reach; how much more so for those things beyond our abilities! And even more amazingly, God is not concerned about the outcome. He Himself determines it! What Hashem cares about is our effort, our readiness to start the task at hand. Moshe Rabbeinu was given credit and was rewarded because he showed readiness to make an effort to erect the *Mishkan*, not because he was actually capable of building it.

Applying effort is essential because it's during this exertion that we build ourselves as people. It's precisely in those moments of hard work and personal investment in an important cause that we strengthen the spiritual muscles responsible for *mesirus nefesh* (self-sacrifice) that stems from a deep love of our fellow Jewish brother or sister. These are the traits that allow us to access the *siyata d'Shmaya* that's required for the true success of any endeavor. Furthermore, we are taught that Moshe actually disassembled and reassembled the *Mishkan* at least twice daily—one time in the morning and once again in the evening. Morning is symbolic of bright times, full of hope and energy. And evening is reflective of the more challenging, difficult times we encounter both personally and nationally. Building, developing, and bettering the world must occur throughout the entire spectrum of human experience.

"But You Are Not Free to Exempt Yourself from It"

> *A student used to come late regularly for Rabbi Shraga Feivel Mendlowitz's 9 a.m. Tanach class. One day, the boy received a notice that the rebbi wanted to speak to him. The boy entered the room trembling.*
>
> *"Nu, Hertzl, when are you going to start coming on time?" Rabbi Shraga Feivel asked. Nervously, the boy had nothing more to say than, "Im yirtzeh Hashem."*

But Rabbi Shraga Feivel was not satisfied with this answer. "Nein,"
*he began, shaking his head. "Not im yirtzeh Hashem, **im yirtzeh**
Hertzl—no, not if Hashem wants; rather, if Hertzl wants!"*[38]

There are times when a person cannot assuage his conscience with
the fact that Hashem runs the world and will take care of what He see
fit. Rather, Hashem is waiting for him to take the initiative. In *Tehillim*
it says, "*Hashem tzilcha al yad yeminecha*—Hashem provides shade over
your right hand."[39] The *Shelah HaKadosh*[40] explains that Hashem is like
our shadow. He will respond and interact with the world in line with
our own efforts and focus. If we strive to cultivate an attitude of doing
and accomplishing, personally and even more broadly, for the greater
good of another Jew or Klal Yisrael, Hashem will be with us and assist
us even if we stumble and do not have enough strength to complete the
task we set out to do. As it says in *Pirkei Avos*,[41] "The work is not upon
you to finish, but you are not free to exempt yourself from it."

Needs Abound

The work that lies ahead of us becomes even more clear when we
observe all the myriad needs that exist today:

- Young men and women are struggling to find their soulmates
  with whom they can build a life together.
- Couples and families are struggling emotionally as well as
  financially.
- *Shalom bayis* and effective parenting are at times overwhelming
  and elusive goals.
- Observant men and women are struggling to fill the outer shell
  of their Jewish lives with inner meaning and real connection.
- Our secular Jewish brothers and sisters are standing on the
  brink of a tidal wave of assimilation, often without even knowing the perilous spot upon which they stand.

---

38   http://www.aish.com/tp/i/gl/117008033.html.
39   *Tehillim* 121:5.
40   *Shnei Luchos HaBris, Shaar HaGadol*, p. 30.
41   *Pirkei Avos* 2:21.

Across the spectrum of Jewish life, within the social, educational, and communal institutions and among individuals, friends, and neighbors, there are great voids but also great talent, skill, and passion. If each person, and especially those with diverse backgrounds, bearing unique abilities and interests, can access their personal warehouse of goods, our communities and the individuals within them will be enhanced and have a chance to flourish.

In *Pirkei Avos* it says: *"B'makom she'ein anashim, hishtadel l'hiyos ish*—in a place where there are no men (i.e., no one standing up to address the challenges at hand), strive to be such a person."[42] The most important and operative word in this Mishnah is *"hishtadel."* We must try, attempt, make an effort. It is not our job and not even possible to ensure the successful outcome of our efforts. Still, we are held accountable and we develop ourselves deeply when we feel responsible to invest what we have to offer to a particular cause or need.

> *The Chafetz Chaim was speaking at a convention of rabbinic leaders at the turn of the twentieth century. He spoke about the waves of assimilation that were threatening the commitment and spiritual health of Jews throughout the world. Afterward, a number of rabbis lamented the great problem he had addressed, but mentioned that they themselves did not feel capable enough to really address it in a way that would make a difference. The Chafetz Chaim overheard this and asked to speak to the assembly again. He told the following story: There was once a man who was traveling from one European city to another and stopped overnight in a particular town. When he requested some water from his host, he was given dirty, sandy water. He questioned his host about this and was told that in this town they hadn't yet learned the process of water filtration. The guest was astounded and went on to teach the man how to filter water. After a few days, the guest left for his intended destination and bid farewell to his grateful host.*

42   *Pirkei Avos* 2:6.

Several months went by and the man who traveled through this particular town met with a person who was originally from there. He inquired as to the well-being of the people he had met on that trip some months back and asked about how things were going. His new acquaintance was incredulous. "You haven't heard?" He proceeded to describe how the entire town had been destroyed in a ravenous fire. "We tried as hard as we could—we were sifting and filtering and sifting and filtering the water as fast as we could, but we just couldn't keep up with the fire, and it completely overtook the entire town."

The Chafetz Chaim stopped there. When there is a fire raging, he explained, you don't stop to look for the purest, most filtered, clean water. Whatever water you have, whatever water you can find, you use. There is a spiritual fire threatening to consume our brothers and sisters. Whatever level each of us is at, and whatever skills we possess, we must use them out there in an effort to save precious souls.

The Giver Gains the Most

Hashem created an amazing phenomenon in the world. One on hand, where there is a void, there is also the voice of Hashem calling on us to bring our whole selves to the table and invest in the Jewish people. But on the other hand, ultimately, we will be the ones who receive the greatest return on that investment. Just like the Talmud records the sage who said: "I have learned much from my teachers and even more from my friends, but from my students I have learned more than from all of them."[43] The teacher learns, benefiting the most from his teaching. So too the giver from his giving. It is those who open their homes, their hearts, and their personal storehouses of talents that gain the most in the process. They experience the deep satisfaction and fulfillment of being an integral and needed part of the fabric of God's world. Developing an other-oriented mentality and becoming a giver shifts the focus from

43   *Taanis* 7a; *Makkos* 10a.

one's own issues and minor frustrations over to others who may lack and need more. It puts things into perspective:

- The single young man or woman will find themselves even slightly less filled with anxiety and feelings of helplessness while waiting to meet their soulmate if, in the meantime, they get involved with their local outreach organization as a tutor or *madrich* (or *madrichah*), or volunteer at their local Chai Lifeline chapter, where their time and skills can be used to provide help that is desperately needed.
- The married couple who experiences the stresses and friction of differing personalities or petty disagreements in opinion and interests will find they can come closer together in the common pursuit of something greater than the two of them. When they open their home for a singles' *Shabbaton*, host an *oneg* for their shul, or invite a new family who moved to the community, they discover a greater appreciation for what they have to give, and through that, for each other.
- We live in a time where people feel burdened by an unprecedented degree of stress, whether financial, emotional, interpersonal, etc. People have to take responsibility for themselves and their lives and make sure they are proactively addressing their challenges. But creating the space to see outside of oneself and direct one's energy toward a cause frees a person from becoming totally consumed by their personal struggles.

A Prerequisite

Of course, a careful balance between giving and taking care of oneself must be created. A person can only give that which he himself has. A cup needs to first be filled in order to overflow and impact its surroundings. A person who is depleted and struggling with major stressors in his own life must first address these in order to establish a baseline state of emotional well-being and healthy functioning. Giving is possible when we take care of our physical, emotional, and spiritual needs. This includes the needs of our spouses and children as well. Our families should not be the *korban*, the sacrificial offering, that is brought upon the altar of *chessed*. First we must strive to build a solid and wholesome foundation for our lives. Then we can carve out time and space for others.

To illustrate, consider the following examples:

- On one hand, the man who always praised those who have guests for Shabbos meals, while excluding himself from the possibility of participating in this special mitzvah opportunity.
- On the other hand, consider the outreach rebbetzin, whose teenage daughter felt her mother had time for every teenage girl who needed her…except for one.

We need to find the middle ground between these two extremes. This dynamic is best described in the wise statement: "*Im ein ani li, mi li, uch'she'ani l'atzmi, mah ani*—If I'm not for myself, who is for me? And if I'm only for myself, then what am I?"[44] In other words, true living happens in the space between how we build ourselves and how we use the self we have created to, in turn, build the world.

---

44   *Avos* 1:14.

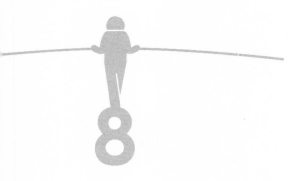

Dating

The Jewish approach to dating is solely marriage-oriented and therefore requires extensive thought and a conscious readiness to engage in something that has such major ramifications for one's life. While not an exhaustive guide to the dating process, this chapter will provide perspective on several points that *baalei teshuvah* commonly confront and need to navigate throughout their dating experiences.

Search Criteria

As individuals decide they are ready to start looking for their soulmate, they will carefully think through the kind of person they feel is best suited for them. They will consider what core values they are looking for in another person, what *hashkafah* within Torah Judaism they are likely to align with, and what types of personality traits might be best. It is likely they will also discuss their criteria with important people in their lives, such as rabbis, rebbetzins, and mentors, and will receive feedback from these individuals on the above points. This is extremely important and often very helpful for individuals as they continually clarify and fine-tune their search in order to be more likely to identify the person that is a right fit for them to build a Jewish home and life with.

However, sometimes *baalei teshuvah* are given the message (whether explicitly or implicitly) by those who guide them that because they, in particular, have shown impressive degrees of growth and integration into their observant surroundings, they are "good enough" to marry a *frum*-from-birth individual. This kind of message is usually not beneficial for the young man or woman seeking clarity in their search for their spouse. First of all, it conveys an underlying message that there is something less than ideal or second-class about being a *baal* or *baalas teshuvah*. Not only is this untrue, it breeds insecurity during a delicate time, where the greatest asset to the individual dating is a solid sense of self and strong self-respect. True confidence in who one is and what they have to offer their potential spouse enables them to remain true to their values and their sense of self-worth. In return, they will be treated with the dignity they deserve from both the people they date and the *shadchanim* and others who attempt to set them up on dates. Any erosion of this confidence can be detrimental and is actually more likely to set the young man or woman back in their dating process rather than help them move forward.

Furthermore, it is simply misguided to create an impression that one should ideally look for a *frum*-from-birth spouse. In some cases, that could be the right choice, but in other cases, not. Ideally, one should seek someone they deeply connect to and can work with as an equally respected partner in building a home in Klal Yisrael, which will reflect their values and life goals. If this individual happens to have grown up observant, there is nothing wrong with this. It is just not what happens most of the time. And for good reason. People are most likely to have mutual understanding with and develop a strong connection to someone they can relate to. They do not need to share every detail in common, but the greater their commonalities, especially in the most significant areas of their lives, the more likely they are to feel the deep camaraderie that is needed as a foundation for building upon.

A young man in his early twenties and shortly out of yeshiva who took on observance several years prior was a star student and held in high regard by all who knew him. He was constantly sent the message that he had really achieved a level that merited an FFB young woman as a wife. He dated one young woman after another, for years, unsuccessful in his search. Finally, someone suggested a woman with a similar background to his. Her family, too, was very secular and she had made the independent choice to take on mitzvah observance in her teenage years, while still in public high school. There were struggles along the way, but much like his own parents, her family accepted her present reality and respected her decisions even if they didn't personally agree with them. Those close to the young man were reluctant, as they felt this would be a step down for a bachur with such refined middos and a love of Torah learning. However, as it had been years of unsuccessful and frustrating dating experiences, they decided not to interfere and the young man accepted this shidduch suggestion. It should not be shocking that a short time later, all were in attendance at this wonderful and very compatible couple's engagement celebration.

It is important to carefully prioritize what one is looking for in a spouse, making sure that the most essential qualities are at the forefront.

A young woman who had recently started the dating process was suggested to a young man who was planning to spend considerable time in full-time kollel learning after getting married. This sounded like a great fit for this young woman, who aspired for the same and was ready to go to great lengths, with mesirus nefesh (self-sacrifice), to make this a possibility for her future marriage. When the parties involved in the match asked if her parents would financially support this young man and their future family in kollel for many years, the young woman laughed.

Her parents were completely unfamiliar with this concept and did not have the means (or intention) to provide this kind of financial support for their adult married children. However, she assured the involved individuals that she was serious and ready to take this responsibility upon herself, and was willing to make sacrifices along the way to make this goal possible for her and her future husband. In return, she was told, "You know, you should feel really lucky that this bachur is still considering you as a potential shidduch. He really could get a girl whose frum parents would be more than happy to support him in kollel for many years." The only lucky thing about this situation was that this young woman possessed enough self-respect to know that her value should not be measured in dollars, social standing, or even yichus. Rather, it would be who she was as a person, her character, depth, spiritual and personal goals, and fortitude at reaching these that would make her future spouse feel honored to share his life with her.

The search for a spouse cannot be a race in conquest of a trophy. A husband or wife is not a status symbol. Truly helpful guidance will reflect a deep acceptance and appreciation of the totality of who a person is and who would be the best match to form a deep and lasting bond with. Whether or not that individual grew up observant should not be a central focus in the dating process.

While similarities in background can often be a strong point in the dating process, *baalei teshuvah* have to also ensure that their prospective spouse is at a current level of observance and overall Jewish development that they feel comfortable with and can respect. Often in dating, a young man or woman will hear their date speak of their goals in Torah growth and the place in their Judaism that they strive to one day reach. While sharing respective goals and dreams, especially with regard to spiritual growth, is a crucial piece in getting to know another person, it is important that in choosing a spouse, you decide to marry the person that they are today, and not the one they hope to become at some point in the future. Being growth-oriented is a major asset and speaks volumes about the character of a person. Even so, a decision can only be made based on the person you see in front of you and where they are now, not where they may or may not be later in life. It can be difficult enough for spouses to make sure that as they respectively grow and develop throughout life, they do so in tandem and as a unit, but to choose to marry someone based on a vision that does not exist in the present reality is risky and likely to set them up for increased disappointment and even regret later in life.

References

If an individual chooses to date through the *shidduch*-style system, where their suggestions for dates will almost always be outside their immediate social circle, it is often encouraged to utilize the references the individual provides to find out preliminary information and determine, based on this, whether or not it makes sense to invest resources, time, and emotional energy to explore this match. In FFB circles, parents will often make these reference calls on behalf of their children. For *baalei teshuvah*, whose parents are not familiar with this process, it can be extremely beneficial to have a trusted and available mentor make reference calls for them. Not only will you benefit from the wisdom and insight they can provide from the information received through the reference calls, you will also feel supported in the dating process itself. Furthermore, it reflects well on an individual that they have mentors who are willing to stand by them and speak on their behalf. It shows that this person is cared for and valued by the important people in their observant lives. This itself is a statement on the degree of growth and integration that this individual has achieved in his or her *frum* life and community. If years go by or if the individual comes to a Torah life as an already settled adult, they may prefer to conduct their own reference inquiries. There is nothing wrong with this. Reference calls are a type of screening process and by no means can replace the dating experience itself. Whatever will bring about an increased sense of dignity, confidence, as well as perspective and insight, is what an individual should choose to do.

A young woman was suggested to a particular yeshiva bachur. After inquiring about her through her teachers and friends, this young man's rebbeim requested to meet with her. She agreed and had a pleasant meeting with one of the rabbis and his wife, where she answered their questions about her background and what she was looking for in a spouse. She discussed this meeting, as well as what she knew about this bachur, with a rabbi who knew her well and whose guidance she trusted. They agreed that it made sense to explore this suggestion and go on a date. But the rebbeim on the young man's side were not quite as ready. They called her again, with further questions about her perspectives on various issues and plans for the future, and they requested another meeting, this time with another rabbi and rebbetzin of this young man. This young woman naturally felt overwhelmed by the degree of investigation she felt she was being put through. Her parents, while supportive and generally involved, didn't have a sense of whether this was normal or not and weren't able to give her much guidance in this particular area. She brought the situation to her rabbi, who was beside himself. "You should not meet with them again. This is too much and it's not right to make you go through all this. If they have any further questions, let them know they can speak to me anytime." The young woman felt great relief. She was able to re-engage and respond to this situation from a place of strength and dignity because she knew she was not alone and had the support base she needed.

Timeframe

Baalei teshuvah may find that as they see their FFB counterparts get engaged after just a handful of dates, they feel pressure to do the same or assume this is what should be the natural outcome of *frum* dating. The average *frum*-from-birth young man or woman will start dating in their early twenties, and while each person is certainly an individual with a unique personality and outlook, their lives may have been relatively simple up until this point. There were likely few major independent decisions made in life thus far. The vast majority of their experiences were within a structured, *frum* environment. This is not a good or bad thing, it simply limits the scope of what this person has been through and the degree to which they have truly formed their adult selves. In fact, many men and women from this background who marry young will find that it is through marriage and family life that they come to a much deeper awareness and understanding of themselves and their needs. Through building their independent lives with their spouse they will come to not only know their partner in new and deeper ways, but themselves as well. While this is true for everyone, it is experienced to a far greater degree for those whose life experiences have been, for the most part, more sheltered and carefully guided by their parents and communal institutions.

Baalei teshuvah, on the other hand, begin the dating phase after a myriad of life experiences that have been thought through, processed, and evaluated. They have made many independent decisions about what they want their lives to look like and have forged paths toward achieving this. Through the process of evaluating society as a whole and the implications on their lives in particular they have come to know themselves in a more sophisticated, developed way. It is then logical that they will need a slightly longer time to express themselves and in turn learn about another person to the degree that they have shared of themselves. There may be more to discuss as well—their journey and the thought processes behind it and how it has changed them as people, among other things. While dating should always remain focused and marriage-oriented, pressure to date for just a few times and be able to determine a lifelong partner who is more complex and mature than some of your peers will hinder, and not help, your ability to reach a decision with a sense of calm and clarity.

How long will it take? However long it needs to take. As long as the dating remains purposeful and a sense of movement is experienced with each date. Remember that Jewish dating is about determining whether you want to be in a relationship with this person and not actually building or enjoying one yet, in this stage. Processing the dating experience with a trusted mentor will be especially helpful in getting objective input that ensures you're on a balanced, healthy path toward finding your spouse.

What to Share and When

With the variety of personal backgrounds and experiences that *baalei teshuvah* bring to their dating, it is important to think through how and when to share important but personal details with the man or woman you are getting to know. While guidance from *daas Torah* is required when asking about and disclosing personal information, and for knowing what is necessary to share and what is not, a few general guidelines may be helpful. Often people want to know sooner rather than later if the person they are dating will accept all the parts of themselves—their past and the experiences that shaped them, along with their current struggles—the residuals of various challenges they encountered as they made their way toward a Torah-observant life. While this is natural, and everyone wants to know that their spouse will accept them fully, it is important to not share indiscriminately, in haste. While it is true that this may require a higher degree of investment of one's time and resources, it is worthwhile. Sharing too much too quickly will leave you vulnerable and often erode your sense of self as you realize you have shared in a way that was not in line with the degree of involvement or seriousness of the relationship at this point. Because this comes from a place of insecurity, it is likely that the man or woman you are seeing will recognize this and will not always respond positively. It is painful to feel that people walk out of your life with parts of yourself that you wish you hadn't handed to them. Instead, evaluate where you are in a given dating relationship. As you get to know each other, open up gradually and be aware of how he or she responds to the things you share about yourself or your life. As you sense increased trust and also seriousness in the relationship, you can and should continue to share on deeper levels. You should know and in turn share all of the "big picture" parts of your life and who you are with the person who will be your spouse. There should be a mutual understanding and appreciation of each other and the experiences that have shaped your lives, both positive and negative. That does not mean you need to, or should, share every detail of past relationships, secular experiences, or struggles, even though the fact that they were a part of your experience will be known. Conversely, it will be counterproductive to pressure the person who may or will be your spouse to share these specifics about themselves. Once there is a thorough, overall sense of who this person is, it should be left to them whether and when they choose to share the specific details of their experiences, especially those that may be more unpleasant or painful to bring up and let another person into. Ideally, both people in a relationship share of themselves out of a desire to connect to another person whom they feel safe with and supported by, rather than from a feeling of pressure to "tell" another person specific sought-after facts.

The Next Step

You are now past the first handful of dates and your conversations are getting more serious. You begin more concretely considering the long-term potential this relationship has. Now is a great time to introduce this young man or woman to one or two rabbis, mentors, or families in the community that you respect and have a close relationship with. Much like introducing a potential spouse to your parents, this is a great way to receive valuable feedback from people who know you well and what you're looking for and need in a husband or wife. These individuals or families will have insight into the areas that are specific to observant life that are particularly core ingredients for the life and home you are looking to build and whether this person seems to be a good fit in those ways. It's also an opportunity for you to evaluate how you feel with this person in public and especially around people you respect and are close to. Do you feel proud to be with him/her? Are you on edge or relaxed around them and the important people in your *frum* life? How you feel with this person around others, and the valuable feedback you receive about your energy and tone together, will be an important factor to consider in your decision-making process.

Leaping

You are at an advanced stage in dating, you feel like you may even be spending time with the person who will be your future husband or wife. You have spent considerable, quality time with one another and enjoy being together. You seem to share core values and a vision of the life you would like to build. You appreciate the qualities you see in him or her and feel that they would make a good, complementary partner to you. Regardless of the fact that they have imperfections that you've been able to pick up on, you respect them and do not feel overwhelmed by the parts that seem less flattering or ideal. It seems like you've checked the major things off your checklist, knowing that you can only focus on your fundamental "needs" and will not get all the "wants." This seems great. But you're still nervous. And the nervousness itself makes you feel more nervous. You wonder if it's normal to feel so nervous. Maybe it's an indicator that marriage is not the next right step here.

Unless you have outlined specific concerns that you've spoken about with objective parties that may be reasons to delay or prevent getting engaged, the general nervous feeling you are experiencing is the fear of leaping. Every single person, whether they realize it or not, is taking a huge leap over a span of countless unknowns when they decide to marry someone. You will never know every eventuality of life with this person. And you are acutely aware of the gravity of the decision you are about to make and its impact on your entire life.

Much like the older child who is afraid to climb a tree, wanting to avoid the pain of falling, while a younger one climbs without fear, a person who is more developed and has more life experience will know more intuitively the pitfalls and challenges that await him as a result of any major decision they make, especially one as big as this. On one hand, if we avoid leaping, we will also block ourselves from the potential to experience deep fulfillment and happiness, even as we protect ourselves in some way by doing so. If you are waiting to know beyond a shadow of a doubt that this is the right person for you to marry, you may wait forever. You may even pass up that very person as you continue to wait for a feeling of certainty. Instead, after checking the person out and thinking things through with your brain—and your "advisors"—choose the one you feel will be a great partner for you, and leap together. There will be unknowns as there always are in life. But your goal will be to become right for each other as you invest your whole selves into the most worthwhile endeavor of your life.

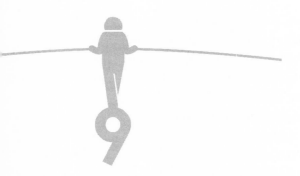

Marriage

The subject of marriage really requires a book of its own. This chapter assumes that the reader has extensive exposure to concepts and ideas that are relevant to the Torah approach to marriage. It is beyond the scope of this book to address this topic thoroughly in a general way. Instead, this section focuses on marriage perspectives that are particularly relevant to *baalei teshuvah*.

Comparisons

Since a *baal teshuvah* did not grow up in an observant family with a *frum* mother or father or older brother or sister, it is likely that the first *frum* male or female role model that a BT had was a rabbi, rebbetzin, or mentor figure of some kind. This person was likely older, married with children, established in his or her family life, as well as in their career or community role. This has several important implications given that most young men and women consciously or subconsciously look for life partners that are similar in many ways to their own parents. In Jewish thought, a Torah teacher has such a far-reaching impact on the student that he or she is likened to a parent. This can be especially true for *baalei teshuvah*, who not only learned about Judaism but also about Jewish living from this individual and their family. Marriage, family life, personal goals, and aspirations all became redefined and then envisioned in a particular way as a result of the relationship we have with the people who role model the life we aspire to create. This is a positive and essential part of Jewish growth, as discussed previously in chapter 2, on what it truly means to *"asei lecha rav."*[45] There is, however, one side effect that can be a potential pitfall for the *baal teshuvah* while dating, and especially as they enter into their own new marriage. There may be a tendency to compare their spouse to that rabbi or rebbetzin that made such a deep impression on them.

Comparison is always lethal in a marriage: Do you really think your spouse is the single smartest, most able, best-looking person on the planet? This type of comparison is particularly counterproductive and unfair to your new husband or wife. We have to keep several factors in mind. Our male or female role model was someone we could not possibly know intimately well, given the nature of our relationship. A young woman who looked up to her rabbi and spent many hours listening to his classes and was a regular at his Shabbos table only saw this individual in his most prepared state, at his best, and in a role that lends itself to the idealization of a person. A person teaching a class and sitting at the head of a Shabbos table full of guests is "on"; he is aware of himself and how he is perceived in these situations. This doesn't mean that he is being insincere but rather that he is consciously putting his best foot forward to inspire and benefit others, as he should be. It's just not the same person who comes home at 6 p.m. on a Tuesday evening, tired after a long day, and is greeted by several tired, grumpy children who are impatiently throwing a variety of requests his way from the moment he enters the house. It's not the same person who finds himself in a disagreement with his wife over their stressful financial situation. We are usually not privy to the less flattering, less prepared moments in

---

45   *Pirkei Avos* 1:6.

other people's lives. To compare our own spouse, who we come to know intimately well and share the ups and downs of life with, to a rabbi/rebbetzin role model is to critique a person's appearance at the beach on a Sunday afternoon next to someone who is entering his car on his way to a black-tie reception where he will deliver the keynote speech for the evening. It is to comment on the blemishes of someone's skin and face when they stand an inch away from us and complain that the person standing across the street seems to have a perfectly smooth, soft, and clear complexion.

Furthermore, we also have no insight into his or her personal development. What was their journey like? What were the things they struggled with that they eventually overcame? What mistakes did they make along the way, as a young single or newlywed, that they learned and grew from? We have to remember that we never knew a *frum* man or woman as they grew into the established adult we see and know. We did not know them as they worked through various insecurities, developed their own *hashkafah*, knowledge base, and skill set. We experienced this person as an already "finished product" to a large degree. When we look at our new husband or wife and feel frustrated or disappointed that they have not yet reached advanced levels of Talmud study or do not seem to be able to manage a baby and a six-course Shabbos meal with a positive attitude, we have to remember we have no idea what our rabbi or rebbetzin, who we feel is doing all this and much more, was like or how well they managed in similar stages and challenges in their own lives.

> *A young woman, shortly out of seminary, got engaged to a young man who had taken on Torah and mitzvos several years prior. When she excitedly called a seminary teacher that she was particularly close with to share the good news, she was surprised by the advice her teacher chose to impart. This teacher was known for her high aspirations and uncompromising attitude in all areas of spiritual growth and accomplishment.*
>
> *"I hear your chassan (fiancé) is a baal teshuvah," she said. "That's good, because if he ever misses minyan or seder, you*

won't have to worry or bother him about it. He chose a life of Torah and mitzvos for himself, after all!" This teacher's wisdom in choosing to model the attitude required for a successful marriage made a lasting impression on her student. Her words showed this new kallah how to search for, and find, the individual greatness of her chassan, without the need to compare him to others or pressure him to "level up" to her role models.

A role model of a Torah marriage and home is an invaluable asset to the creation of your own marriage and family. But it is imperative to develop the awareness that while comparisons of our spouse to our role models may be natural and common, they can easily become destructive forces in our marriages.

Leveraging Our Resources

Often, *baalei teshuvah* underutilize one of the greatest assets they have in creating their own happy and successful marriages—the healthy, positive marriage of their parents! If, growing up in our homes, we witnessed a positive, healthy example of marriage, it is a great blessing and can be the most powerful tool as we embark on building our own. Emotional health and well-being, mutual respect, deep friendship, and other aspects of a strong marriage are certainly fundamental to Torah values and Torah life but are not inherently related to Torah observance. If our parents' marriage role modeled these characteristics, we should consciously utilize their example and allow it to influence and shape our own marriage for the better.

On the other hand, if we did not see an example of a healthy marriage growing up, it may seem that this skill or achievement is somehow "outside" of ourselves. This is a natural feeling since integrated knowledge often comes from life experience rather than intellectual information or facts alone. If the marriage we saw growing up was not a healthy or sustainable one, we need to recognize that and embark on the difficult task of identifying what types of behaviors and patterns contributed to it, enabling ourselves to consciously developer a healthier, more positive approach. Part of this thought process will entail determining the degree to which your parents will be involved in the details of your personal life. Relationship bumps, financial stressors, or challenges in raising children are all common phenomena and should be expected as part of married life. Each couple will have to make the decision whether or not input and advice from family members who did not themselves succeed in these areas should be accepted or given serious consideration. Instead, a couple will need to focus on ways to give their marriage the input it needs from the sources that will allow it to thrive and be successful.

Reading books and going to classes on marriage will give the couple important theoretical concepts but is also likely to be the tip of the iceberg for truly integrating the skills needed to create a positive, Torah-true marriage. Ideally, young men and women establish several real-life role models of good and healthy marriages well before they are responsible for this task themselves. This role may be taken on by one's rabbi or rebbetzin—but it does not have to be. It needs to be a couple or family that personifies the Torah values and attitudes that are inherent to building a strong relationship. There are obvious limitations to how much we can be privy to witnessing another person's relationship, but as long as the family seems authentic and sincere, it can be a great way to gather real-life insights into what a strong marriage looks like and how it functions.

> *A young woman in her mid-twenties reflects on a particular moment she feels redefined her expectations for marriage. She recalls many years ago, as a teenager who was active in her NCSY chapter, that she spent many Shabbosim at the home of a family she became close with after they hosted her and several friends during a Shabbaton weekend. She thinks back to one particular Friday night, when, just prior to the guests arriving, the couple was discussing which sodas to put out for the meal. The wife chose one type of soda and the husband another. Neither felt that both drinks were necessary, as there would also be water and juice on the table. But since each of them clearly preferred a specific type of soda, they decided it didn't*

really matter that one bottle would be extra; they would put both out. This is a simple and seemingly completely insignificant exchange between spouses. It doesn't even begin to touch on the fundamental and often stressful issues that couples need to address in marriage and family life. And yet, this young woman remembers standing near their kitchen stunned. "That's it?" she asked incredulously. The couple couldn't understand what she meant at first. She went on to explain that in her home, even the slightest difference of opinion or confrontation would result in a full-out battle. It was the first time in her life that she realized that constant tension and aggression were not an inherent part of marriage.

When observing couples who seem to role model a successful marriage, try to look beyond the *divrei Torah* at the Shabbos table and other overt practices of the family. Rather, notice the smaller, more nuanced moments in between, such as how they respond to a misbehaving child, how they manage minor disagreements that come up between them, or how they act with one another on a Monday night, or Shabbos afternoon, or during the carpool rush to or from school. As long as they are comfortable with it, try and spend time with their family and in their home frequently, and consciously take note of the feel and tone of the environment there, in order to learn from them. Offering to babysit or otherwise help in their home can be one way to facilitate a deeper and more intimate connection to them than being present at their Shabbos table. Many *baal teshuvah* singles opt to seek out boarding options by warm and welcoming families in their communities. Even if they are financially capable of living independently, it can be a deeply enriching experience to be part of an observant home before taking personal responsibility for building one. These individuals often feel more confident and equipped to embark on their own marriage and family journey, having developed a more integrated sense of what this looks like in real life.

Once a couple, where one or both of the spouses comes from less-than-ideal or unhealthy home environments, is married and actively creating their own relationship and home, they have to build consciously, and actively make decisions regarding their married life, not relying on their upbringing to provide them with the tools they need for this task. While couples from intact and healthy families seem able to begin their own marriages with the know-how they received through osmosis, the couple who does not have this luxury needs to attempt this in a more conscious way. When both spouses embark on this as a team, it can be a great way to facilitate a sense of closeness and intimacy between them. One way to do this is through setting relationship goals together as a couple. Another way is to consciously recognize and discuss each of your respective strengths that you both feel significantly contribute to your marriage. This will facilitate mutual respect as well as actively build your relationship in specific areas. For example, your husband or wife may be very timely or especially considerate of others. Use him or her as your teacher for those *middos*. In addition to fostering your respect for your spouse, this will give you a small glimpse into understanding why Hashem specifically brought this person into your life to expand you in certain ways.

Not only do we want our marriages to thrive on an emotional level, we also want to make sure our marriage is growing and thriving on a spiritual level as well. Working through *hashkafic* ideas and issues together, even if we ultimately agree that we need to consult with our rabbi about a particular issue, will strengthen our bond to both our Judaism and to one another. This is perhaps why learning through a Torah book or Jewish topic together that both spouses find interesting is commonly encouraged for couples. It allows the couple to grow in their Judaism together. Their Jewish journey, which up until this point had been deeply personal and individualistic, is now meant to be shared and developed jointly. Growing together spiritually is a great formula for growing together as a couple.

Boundaries

In addition to maintaining a connected and growing dynamic between spouses, the establishment of boundaries around a marriage is another essential ingredient to a solid and healthy relationship. The concept of boundaries is regularly rejected by the secular world. It has become one of the least popular notions in modern-day society. Boundaries are essential because they keep in, restrain, filter, and protect. The broader society in which we live emphasizes breaking through limitations and going against established norms in favor of indulging uninhibited, instinctive behavior. In other words, boundaries are seen as negative, limiting forces in life that hold us back from doing, saying, and being whatever we want. In this social climate, it is unpopular to have parts of one's life that are not publicly displayed or discussed.

Yet, in contrast, *tzniyus*, modesty, is a Torah value that creates an inner, private world, thereby facilitating dignity. A Torah marriage is one where the dignity of each spouse and of the relationship as a whole is carefully preserved. Furthermore, Judaism gives *shalom bayis*, or harmony between spouses, precedence over many other things, including objective facts and observations. This is because marriage is considered holy and a distinct unit, taking priority over the two individuals involved as its ability to thrive is seen as vital to nurture and sustain each of them.

For example, it is customary to elaborate on the strengths and positive qualities of the bride and groom at each of the *sheva berachos*, the post-wedding celebratory meals that are hosted for them. The words spoken in their honor, while not untrue, may often be slightly embellished or exaggerated. This is because endearing one spouse to the other is more important than his or her exact IQ, or how actually beautiful or attractive he or she is according to society's standards, etc. While in dating objectivity and even a degree of scrutiny of the other's qualities and traits is emphasized, once a couple is married, all this should fade into a mutual acceptance and consciously positive outlook toward one another. This is in contrast to broader society, which increasingly sees marriage as a less preferable, but at times unavoidable state (note the notion of a bachelor party in the secular world). This creates a very haphazard attitude that can pervade the dynamic between spouses and among friends.

Since Torah ideas are so antithetical to the mentality of secular society, it is likely that the broader base a couple has of involved family and friends, the harder they will have to work to establish healthy and appropriate boundaries as a couple. Immediate and extended family and well-meaning friends may ask prying questions regarding the details of the couple's intimate life, or they may make jokes to one spouse that in some way demean or degrade the other. They may even directly comment on a negative trait or behavior of one of the spouses. Likely, none of this will be done in malice. But it is no less destructive to a marriage. A couple will have to consciously create a tone for their relationship and present as a united front to the world. This will apply to how others treat and talk about their spouse. As a rule, disparaging or negative words about one's spouse, regardless of whether they are true or not, should never be tolerated. This is certainly not referring to abusive situations or tendencies where people are trying to sincerely be an objective source of reason or help to the individual. But outside of that scenario, even well-intentioned critiques, jokes, or "suggestions" that in some way put down your spouse should be confronted and effectively shut down. Loving and well-meaning family and friends need to know that there is no room to share their criticisms of your spouse.

> *A recently married baalas teshuvah was approached by a cousin at a family dinner. She and her husband were married for several months and had made the decision to start off their marriage with her husband learning full-time in kollel. Her cousin approached her and smiled sweetly but sighed. "You know, we just all think so highly of you. You're so beautiful and so smart, we really think you deserve someone who would be successful in his career."*
>
> *The young woman smiled back and immediately made it known that she couldn't be happier with the choices she and her husband had made in their new life together and that she feels blessed to have found such a quality person to spend her life with.*

That conversation was over. Contrast that scenario with another, very similar one.

Another young wife, only a year into her marriage, had already heard countless times from her mother how short and generally unkempt her new husband was and how unfortunate this was. This young woman allowed these comments to continue and they naturally marinated and developed in her own mind. It is not surprising that this couple struggled with affection and intimacy, among other things.

The balance between creating and maintaining positive, friendly relationships with family and friends and creating an expectation of respect for each spouse and their boundaries as a couple is one of the most crucial things for a couple to navigate.

Managing Expectations

In addition to the balance that exists in the relationships the couple has with others, there is another important balance that must be struck. That is the inner dynamic of the couple, in the relationship between the two spouses. When a couple gets married, they consciously or subconsciously bring with them many expectations about who their spouse will be and what kind of home they will build together. For *baalei teshuvah*, a lot of this is heavily influenced by the people who they looked to for guidance in building an observant life, as discussed previously. Taking with us the inspiration, guidance, and aspirations we developed as we grew as people and as Torah Jews, we have to be careful to remain a committed, dear partner and friend to our spouse rather than their coach or employer, taking careful note of a job well done or areas where there is less optimal performance. This works best if we remember to keep the focus on our own obligations and goals within a marriage and not teaching our spouse about theirs.

In reality, keeping track of a spouse's performance is a reflection of a secular viewpoint of marriage, where marriage is a means for one to fulfill their own needs and desires with a partner who is expected to help them accomplish this. A Jewish marriage is one where each spouse learns from the other to become a more complete and whole person themselves, all the while seeing God's hand in bringing this person into their life and how they complement the life they are striving to build.

Along with a certain portrayal of a *frum* husband or wife, we also developed an image of what our *frum* family would be like.

> *I still remember, years later, my seminary principal making the statement in one of our classes that baalei teshuvah have a hard time establishing a frum home successfully. Since I was the only baalas teshuvah in the school, I was the only one who was extremely shocked by the comment. After class, I approached him for clarification. I couldn't accept failure at a task I hadn't yet attempted, in addition to the great investments I felt I was making toward the very goal of a strong, vibrant, and enduring Torah-true home. He asked me, rhetorically, "When you picture your future home, do you envision guests all the time for Shabbos? Zemiros being sung throughout the meal? Divrei Torah all the time, at every meal?"*
>
> *I thought about it. In fact, it was somewhat similar to what I was envisioning. And then, one of the most important lessons for life registered with me. Our home cannot be a stage where family members feel the need to "perform." Rather it should be a place that is a fertile ground for the innate kochos of individuals to develop and flourish. This place needs to be accepting, warm, and gently directing. It needs to be a place that is in line with reality and simultaneously striving for greatness. It should be comfortable, not pressurizing or overly idealized. Of course, divrei Torah and zemiros and hachnasas orchim are all wonderful, important aspects of our Shabbos experience. We just want to be careful to make sure these come naturally and without too much pressure. I thought back to a Shabbos meal I had recently been at and the discomfort I felt when the family members, from eldest to youngest, took turns reciting cued zemiros and pre-planned speeches on the parashah. It felt contrived, overly planned, and while beautifully and perfectly orchestrated, unpleasant and too formal for a family. It was more like being in a theater than a Shabbos table at someone's home. I wanted the home, not the stage.*

My principal was sending the message that building a home is the result of who a person is and not what they demand of others in that home. Unrealistically high expectations will only obstruct the ideals we have for our homes.

Impacting One Another

On the other hand, it is equally important to recognize the enormous potential we do have in influencing our spouses and families. This is not exclusive to the "Jewish" areas of life, e.g., influencing each other to learn more, dress more in line with higher standards of modesty, daven more regularly, etc. Rather, spouses should be aware of the great potential they have to deeply build up one another as individuals, allowing them greater ability for success in all areas of life.

The Torah uses the word *"va'yiven,"* literally translated as "and he built," to describe the creation of Chavah, the first woman.[46] Chavah's creation held deep implications for the inherent makeup and potential of all femininity. Women would not only go on to become builders of humanity and society, but there would be something about building that would define her internal reality, the way she approaches life and responds to her surroundings.

The root letters of *"va'yiven"*[47] are *vav, nun, hei,* which spell the word *"binah."* Binah, commonly understood as intuition, is the ability to extrapolate one thing from another, to see the bigger picture at play in a given situation, to take one experience or encounter and build a deep understanding or insight into the people behind it. *Binah* is the ability to see stress and anxiety in a child who arrives home from school in a grumpy, aggressive mood. It's the ability to be calm and exhibit patience with this child rather than conduct a lesson on better manners or character development. *Binah* is the ability to sense how your husband's day went after he offers a one- or two-word response to your inquiry upon his arrival home. *Binah* is the capacity to recognize potential, to see latent skills and abilities, and also the sense of how to best bring

46   *Bereishis* 2:22.
47   *Niddah* 45b.

those to fruition. When women tap into the power of their *binah*, when they listen to the quiet inner voice of intuition, they have the potential to influence and inspire in transformative ways. When a wife shows her husband the version of himself that she sees he is capable of reaching, the version that she admires and respects, it gently but powerfully inspires him to develop into that person.

As the one in the relationship who has a direct mitzvah to learn Torah, a husband has an equally significant impact on his wife. Through his constant focus on growth in his Torah learning and character development, he infuses his home with energy and idealism. By seeking out Torah opportunities that serve as a focal point for his life, be it a *shiur*, *chavrusa*, or *beis midrash* environment, he provides his family with a direct link into the world of Chazal and great rabbis throughout the generations. When the children ask their mother where their father is and she replies with pride that he went to learn Torah, they have the opportunity to taste the beautiful dynamic of a Jewish marriage, where husband and wife both contribute to each other and to the family as a whole.

Influence between spouses in a marriage is not only inevitable but can provide an incredible gift of growth and development. If it is done with love and encouragement rather than out of pressure, comparisons to others, and exceedingly high expectations, it is something to embrace and welcome as part of the relationship.

Intimacy

One final area of marriage that *baalei teshuvah* sometimes need tailored guidance in navigating, or orienting to, is intimacy. Discussing a Torah approach to intimacy is most effective in an in-person setting, with a trusted rabbi, rebbetzin, or Torah teacher. That is why, despite intimacy being a topic that deserves lengthy discussion, as it is crucial to building a strong, Torah-true marriage, it will only be mentioned relatively briefly in this book. All young men and women who are about to embark on the journey of marriage and creating their own *bayis ne'eman b'Yisrael* need guidance as to the proper Torah approach to intimacy. *Baalei teshuvah* specifically often have to make a mental switch from the exploited and degraded form of physicality that is pervasive within the secular culture, to the very positive and *kadosh* expression it is meant to have within a Torah marriage. As *baalei teshuvah* take on observance, especially women, they find that as difficult as certain mitzvos, such as *shomer negiah, yichud,* and *tzniyus* are, these very same things offer a type of dignity and safety that cannot be found in the secular world. They come to experience the power that these mitzvos have in presenting us to the world as a person first and a body second. They begin to identify with their inner worth and appreciate that these mitzvos demand that same recognition from the people they interact with. Furthermore, many come to a Torah life with the scars of experiences that left them hurt and their sense of self-worth depleted. Judaism says that physicality is extremely powerful. As with anything powerful, the degree to which it can be used for the bad is also the degree to which it can be harnessed and experienced for the good. Just like nuclear energy can be utilized to provide power and light to an entire city, it can likewise be misused to destroy an entire city. The Torah goes to great lengths to guard expressions of intimacy in such a way that they can be utilized to build the deepest connection and love between spouses, and ultimately bring the Shechinah, God's presence itself, into their marriage.[48] To experience this, couples need to be taught the beauty and holiness that is inherent in this powerful aspect of human nature that Hashem created.

Becoming a Well

Rav Shlomo Wolbe[49] quotes the *pasuk: "Shesei mayim mi'borecha v'nozlim mitoch be'ercha*—drink water from your pit and liquid from your well,"[50] and brings a source from the *Zohar* that explains it to mean that one of the greatest opportunities and missions of life is to transform oneself from a pit, which has no merits on its own and can only receive from others, into a wellspring. Rav Wolbe goes on to say that this great goal can be accomplished specifically through marriage and building a

---

48   *Sotah* 17a.
49   Rav Wolbe, *Maamarei Hadrachah L'Chassanim*, p. 8.
50   *Mishlei* 5:1.

home, as the couple creates an environment that is truly self-sufficient and depends on no one else.

We are taught that many of our forefathers and great people who contributed to building the foundation of the Jewish people met their future wives at a well. Perhaps one of the insights we can glean from this is that a marriage, like a well, should be the source of one's needs. Just like a well nourishes and provides for people, so too a marriage should sustain and nourish the basic needs of each spouse. This doesn't mean that spouses must have all the same interests of hobbies, or that they will never need input and support from outside sources. Rather, it implies that the deepest, most fundamental needs of both individuals in that relationship—a sense of being needed and appreciated, physically and emotionally desired, and of contributing to the building of the Jewish people, etc.—are found and enjoyed within the relationship itself.

A Jewish home has the capacity to become a place that sustains the lives of the individuals who dwell within it, as well as contributing spiritual, emotional, and other nourishment outside of itself to fellow Jews who lack these essentials. The spiritual architects, builders, and interior designers—the nucleus of that home—are the husband and wife who invest themselves into building an enduring, warm, and nourishing space.

10

Parenting

etween carpool, homework help, extracurricular activities, managing sibling rivalry, discipline, and more, it's easy to forget what we are actually trying to do as parents. What is the big picture here? What is our overriding parenting goal?

Imagine holding one lit candle to another, unlit candle. You put the lit flame gently next to the wick of the second candle. And you wait. Slowly, the wick catches fire and it begins to glow on its own. You move your candle back and enjoy the two beautiful flames lighting up the darkness, side by side.

Parenting has the potential to be a magical process, a transfer of rich heritage and legacy, of spiritual identity and personal purpose. Beyond providing for their physical needs, as parents we give our children crucial information about who they are, their capacity for contribution to the world, and the initial tools they will need to develop themselves. Eventually, they begin to stand independently, deeply impacted by our flame and yet able to shine on their own. Our goal is to build another solid link in the chain of the Jewish people from Har Sinai and toward the future, to have such a deep and lasting impact on another person that it influences how they go on to impact the world in their own right. This implies that while a pleasant relationship with our children is a critical means to the end, and perhaps the only way to accomplish our ultimate goal, it is not itself the overriding goal of our job as parents.

A Dying Art

Parenting is perhaps the greatest example of a dying art in our society today. There is a popular anecdote that is told about a rabbi traveling on an airplane. The man sitting next to him notices that this rabbi's grandson is constantly checking on his grandfather to make sure he is comfortable and has everything he needs. The young boy repeatedly brings the rabbi drinks and food and chats pleasantly with him throughout the course of the flight. At some point, the rabbi's neighbor can no longer hold back his curiosity.

"I don't understand," he begins, incredulous. "My grandson will barely speak to me, much less tend to my needs! He thinks I'm old fashioned and outdated. What did you do to have your grandson show you such respect and positivity?"

The rabbi explains that it's actually quite simple. He tells his neighbor, "Your grandchildren believe you descended and evolved from monkeys. So the older you are, the closer you are to being a monkey. My grandkids believe we descended from Abraham, Isaac, and Jacob, holy and wise people. In their eyes, the older a person is, the closer they are to greatness." This story is not a refutation of evolution. It is a reflection of a prevalent attitude of our time.

We live in a culture that worships youth. With rapid technological advancements, combined with a growing negative sentiment toward tradition, established values, morals, or norms, the people who can master the newest gadgets, social media, or pop-culture references the fastest are seen as respectable and impressive. The wisdom that is borne of experience and passed down through a rich heritage are scorned and undermined. Parents are seen as outdated and irrelevant at best. At worst, they are considered a barrier in the way of their children's progressive views and entitled desires. This sentiment has run so deep that parents have begun to see themselves this way! It is not uncommon to see parents ridiculing themselves in front of their children, commenting on their own lack of tech savvy or trying to mimic their kids' style of dress and speech, all just reinforcing their kids' views that their parents really don't have much to offer.

The reality, however, is that our children need parents who are actively parenting more than ever before. In previous generations, people relied heavily on intergenerational connections and their insular communities to support and supplement their efforts in child raising. The values, moral standards, and expectations of the community were often homogenous and reflective of the families that constituted any given community. Even the secular world, while always at odds in some ways with Torah values and outlook, upheld a certain standard of decent behavior and moral expectations of its citizens.

The climate in which our children are growing up today is quite different. Extended families live spread across the world. Our schools and communities are facing unprecedented financial and spiritual challenges. They can offer some positive supplementation to the upbringing we strive to provide our children, but cannot be held responsible for carrying the main burden. In our broader society, moral relativism and an abandonment of authority of any kind is prevalent. There are few places for our children to glean wisdom, obtain guidance, and develop the necessary tools with which to build an emotionally, physically, and spiritually healthy and successful life. It is crucial that our home and our relationship with our children become this most-needed place. A place of love, support, identity, and direction. Our kids need our wisdom, our guidance, and our strength. They desperately need capable parents in order to grow into capable adults. They need us to be secure in our abilities, to instill within them much-needed confidence of their own. Even as children grow older and, at times, show outward resentment at our directives or discipline, they deeply crave the structure and support these provide.

The Newcomer's Challenge

Baalei teshuvah frequently feel under-equipped to provide this guidance in a system that they themselves have never navigated. They may feel unfamiliar with the social and educational norms in their community. It may be especially difficult to feel confidence in their abilities as parents when, frequently, their children may come to "know" more than they do in certain areas of Judaism. In some ways, this experience is not unlike that of an immigrant to a new country. There will be things they learn through and alongside their children. However, that still does not have to erode at their fundamental sense of security in their abilities as parents. *Baalei teshuvah*, like all Jews, should try to constantly grow in Torah knowledge and familiarity. Still, even if one's children know a specific phrase, story, or concept that the parents do not, they must remember that they bring decades of life experience, wisdom, and general knowledge to the table that enhance and deepen any basic information children may bring home from school. A parent should never feel beneath or secondary to their children as a result of a gap in technical information or knowledge. Instead, they can instill a sense of pride into their children that they have parents who, like Avraham Avinu, were critical thinking enough to question and had enough inner fortitude to take a stand against the norms and values of their society. Avraham Avinu is called "Ha'Ivri" because he stood alone in his intellectual honesty, opposing the entire world with its immorality, embracing Torah and *emunah* amid great difficulty. This is something to truly be proud of.

It Starts with You

That being said, the only way your children will feel that pride is if you feel it first. If you truly recognize the greatness that is reflected by your independent choices and self-propelled growth, then your children will deeply feel this way as well. In those moments where you do not have an answer to a specific question that your child asks, instead of giving them an answer, you can give them something even greater—a living example of the greatness of being a lifelong student. All Jews are obligated to learn Torah. There is no graduation date. There is no limit to the infinite wisdom contained within it that we strive to acquire to whatever extent we can. Your child will see you as a person who continually strives to expand and deepen their Torah knowledge. And your child will have a greater chance of one day seeing him or herself this way as well.

My husband once attended a shiur by a well-known Rosh Yeshiva. During the shiur, several pressing questions were raised about the educational system in our times. After the shiur, my husband approached the Rosh Yeshiva, eager to hear the answers to these questions that had been raised but were not answered during the class.

The Rosh Yeshiva laughed and said, "You want me to give you an answer to these questions? There are some questions I've been walking around with for forty years!" The Rosh Yeshiva ended up giving my husband and the entire group something significantly more meaningful than an answer to even the greatest question. He gave them the sense that questioning, actively thinking through ideas and issues, even when no clear answer is available, is what being Jewish is really all about.

It is the process that deeply builds who we are, and ultimately matters more than the outcome or end goal. Some issues can't be easily resolved; many questions do not have quick answers. Rather, being an engaged and proactive member of the Jewish people is what creates the positive impact that is needed in the world.

Baalei teshuvah may also experience increased feelings of insecurity at the various stages and life-cycle moments in their children's lives that are specific to the experience of children growing up in observant homes. Entering the day-school system, preparing a child for bar or bas mitzvah and then hosting a *simchah* to mark the occasion, guiding children as they enter adolescence, and then as they begin *shidduchim* and eventually enter into a Torah marriage of their own, may all feel like hurdles that are too tall to scale. It is especially during these times that *baalei teshuvah* have to carefully balance seeking advice about what is considered standard in their surroundings as well as how to manage these situations in the most ideal way, combining common sense with thoughtful calculation of what would be best for their particular child. There is nothing wrong with gathering facts and learning new ways of handling the issues that present themselves at various stages in life. As long as a parent does not negate themselves, their inherent wisdom, and the fundamental respect that they deserve from their children, these new experiences, while challenging, can be eye-opening and facilitate growth. In fact, the greater the parent's degree of confidence in their own abilities to navigate even new situations, the greater their likelihood for both success in the endeavor and a renewed sense of trust from their child.

Unconditional Love

There is a delicate balance that must be struck, where, on one hand, we develop and teach respect by enforcing rules and expectations about how to speak and act toward a parent, while, on the other hand, ensuring that we never become tyrannical or overbearing in demanding more than a child is capable of giving or doing. We want to make sure we create space for a casual and warm relationship between parent and child. This is the fertile ground on which we plant our ideals, values, and direction for life. Our children need to know and feel that our love for them is unconditional, not dependent on their behavior, performance, degree to which they reflect our own hopes and dreams for them, or any other factor. There is a huge difference in criticizing behavior as opposed to the person. When our children experience any disapproval from us, it should be clear that it is directed at a specific behavior or shortcoming, and does not define who they are or their overall standing in our eyes and hearts.

Extended Family

Baalei teshuvah will inevitably have to deal with explaining their background and their family's differing level of observance to their children. It is likely that children as young as four or five years old will begin to notice and ask questions about why Grandma and Grandpa dress differently than other *bubbies* and *zeidies*, or why they can't eat at their house, among other questions relating to the lack of mitzvah observance that they notice in the lives of their grandparents or other extended family members. A great rule of thumb in these situations is to be honest without denigrating. Our children need to trust us as reliable sources of information and guidance in many areas of life. In order to retain this trust, we have to respond to them and their questions in an honest and direct way. They also have to develop a sense of pride in where they come from. Their grandparents are an integral part of this broader context and identity. Still, honesty does not have to come at the expense of conveying respect and dignity for our family, and by extension, ourselves. Honesty also does not imply oversharing and providing information that is extraneous and unnecessary. For young children, it will be enough to respond to their questions simply—"Grandma and Grandpa don't keep Shabbos because they don't know about Torah and mitzvos," or "Grandpa doesn't wear a *kippah* because he was never taught to do so." They are not bad people, or negative forces to be around. They simply do not know better. It is unnecessary to go into detail about exactly how Grandma and Grandpa break Shabbos or what types of food they enjoy while eating in *treif* restaurants.

Often, parents will worry that their nonobservant parents will stir their children's curiosity in spiritually harmful ways. We have to remember that a child's immediate home environment carries with it the most significant impact on their values and standards. Following up on questions related to secular family with "We are so lucky that we did get to learn about Torah and mitzvos" is a good way to convey a sense of pride and satisfaction in living a Torah way of life. Children's interest will only be piqued if they sense a degree of excitement or longing in our voice as we talk about the nonkosher food or experiences we once had or that our families still partake in. Relaying (appropriate) facts in a neutral way alone will not sway a child in one direction or another. If we make sure our own interests and sense of satisfaction lies within Jewish life, we will not have to worry that witnessing some behavior to the contrary from grandparents or others will deeply impact our children. The only instances where parents have to directly confront involved family members about their differing behavior is if they see these individuals speaking in front of the children in ways that belittle or otherwise tear down the Torah values and behaviors that are being inculcated into a home.

As children get older, these same conversations will happen but at more mature and sophisticated levels. Here, for example, parents may explain why even though someone technically "knows" something (since grandparents will, at minimum, know about various parts of Torah observance through their children and grandchildren) they don't respond to that information by integrating it into their lives and outlooks. Love and compassion toward your family and a sense of confidence and excitement about your decisions to embark on a life of Torah and mitzvos will serve to keep these conversations productive and meaningful. This process can broaden one's child in positive ways and also instill the notion that you as their parent are a great source of guidance and perspective as they navigate the world around them.

Erecting Fences

Rav Wolbe[51] compares parenting to "planting," cultivating fertile soil through love, warmth, and connection, and then "building," embedding all the lessons, messages, and directives needed for the identities of those who will grow in our garden. Planting a beautiful garden requires a fence to keep out animals, careless pedestrians, and other potential outside forces that bring danger and pose potential risk to our garden and its ability to grow to full fruition. In that sense, we need to be sensitive to the fact that the majority of the Torah values, standards, and ideas that we are trying to instill within our children are not reflected and often not even understood or respected by the broader society in which we live. This is not a new phenomenon in Jewish history. The Gemara teaches: "*Chochmah b'goyim taamin, Torah b'goyim al taamin.*"[52] With this statement, the Gemara is guiding us toward making an important distinction: If someone tells you that there is wisdom among the nations of the world, you should believe them. There is important information, discoveries, and advancements in medicine, technology, science, and most areas of life that the world at large is producing. We should not ignore this and do not have to deny it. However, Torah—morality, a value system, a way to understand how to interpret the facts and findings, how to engage with the information, and how to behave as a result of any societal advancement—is impossible to find in the world at large.

---

51   Rav Shlomo Wolbe, *Zeriah U'Binyan B'Chinuch* (Jerusalem: Feldheim, 1995), p. 12.
52   *Eichah Rabbah* 2:13.

Only Torah itself can be the ultimate guide for our values and views on the issues that arise in any society, at any time throughout history. Misguided use of the world is spiritually destructive. We need to be aware of what media, experiences, and conversations our children are being exposed to and build fences when necessary.

> *A couple with children spanning the ages of two through thirteen was intensely involved with an outreach organization and frequently hosted secular students in their home for Shabbos meals. They felt comfortable having individuals with various backgrounds and varying levels of observance in their home and involved with their family because they felt confident in their abilities to manage and guide conversations and interactions that happened within the sphere of their home environment. On the other hand, when this organization would host Shabbatonim in hotels or other remote locations, they would give serious consideration to whether they would take any of their children along for the weekend. When hosting secular guests within their own home, this couple felt there was a positive pressure to behave in accordance with standards that exist in an observant home. Away from home and in an environment significantly less structured, their children could be exposed to language or behavior that could negate the very sensitivities their parents sought to instill.*

> *Another baal teshuvah couple would attend extended family celebrations and events frequently in an effort to maintain a positive and close relationship with relatives. But when these events would take place in treif restaurants with a bar, live music, and dancing, they made sure to excuse their children from attendance.*

Protecting the garden is a necessity. We cannot expect flowers to bloom in an unhealthy environment.

On the other hand, we cannot be so terrified of the "dangers" that surround us that we cripple our children's ability to navigate the outside world while remaining true to their standards and ideals. It is naive to assume our children will never have to come in contact with broader society and its messages in one form or another. In a world that has been made smaller and more interconnected than ever, it is unrealistic to hope than we can insulate our homes from penetration of any kind from the outside world.

There are a variety of ways to respond to the challenges that we and our children face in our modern society, only some of which will prove successful in raising a generation of strong and committed Jews. Rabbi Yaakov Horowitz[53] gives the analogy of the prospect of a Walmart opening up down the block from a small mom-and-pop shop that services their local community's needs. This small family business is threatened by the potential arrival of the mega-store and has a few options of what they can do to address this situation:

- One possibility is that they become paralyzed by fear, living in denial of Walmart's arrival. In this case, they do nothing, while speaking disparagingly of the general increase in large stores, hoping that somehow they will not be impacted by the inevitable.
- The other possibility is that the owners of this small store will begin to brainstorm, to proactively strategize how to address this new competition. How will they stay in business and retain their customer base in light of this threat? How can they provide their customers with something that Walmart cannot? This type of thinking is offensive instead of defensive. It will tackle issues head on and address them instead of hoping the challenge won't be too overwhelming or cause irrevocable damage.

In our world, Walmart is not only coming, it is already here. Whether it is through technology, billboards in the streets, or in the workplace as young adults, our children, even in insular communities, will inevitably come in contact with material, ideas, and experiences that are

53   Rabbi Yaakov Horowitz, *Living and Parenting* (New York: Mesorah Publications Ltd, 2008), p. 225.

antithetical to Torah values and standards. We need to equip our children with their own ability to be strong when their identities will be challenged. This means assertiveness rather than fear will be our modus operandi. "How will they manage?" instead of "How can they hide?" will be the question to answer. When they see, hear, or question something, instead of responding in fear and shutting down the experience, we can engage our children in a productive conversation around the issues and help them build their own internal navigation system to manage the complexities of the world we live in. Children whose parents were actively involved in guiding them through various exposures to the secular world will be far more equipped and capable as adults who encounter these same things on their own, later in life.

The circumstance of a ten-year-old child of *baalei teshuvah* who encounters secular cousins who question why he wears a *kippah* or can't go out to eat with them can either be viewed as threatening or as an opportunity. Such a situation can be utilized to instill pride in who we are, reinforce why we do what we do, and strengthen a sense of security in that which makes us different. A child can walk away more confident than he was prior to entering that situation when he is able to confront something different from him and not feel threatened by it. This same child will grow into a young adult who is unfazed by most interactions with the non-Jewish world in his work environment and in the technologies and media he will use as an inevitable part of functioning in today's world.

If we produce children who are so weak that any encounter is a possible threat to their spiritual existence, we are not succeeding in our role. While we need to monitor and guide our children through the experiences they have, we do not need to fear or resist all of them automatically. It will be our strength in confronting issues in our society that will create strong children who become solidly rooted adults. When Yosef HaTzaddik finds himself alone in the most depraved place on earth as a seventeen-year-old boy, he struggles with an enormous test. As he battles with himself internally and tries to resist being seduced by immorality, there is one factor that gives him the strength to succeed: the image of his father, Yaakov Avinu. Having an awareness of the values and lessons of his father, and deeply connecting to these, Yosef was able to find his own inner fortitude in times of struggle and opposition. Also, we see an interesting thing in the blessings we give our children on Friday night. We bless our sons to grow up to be like Ephraim and Menasheh. But why do we not bless them to be like the *Avos* or Yosef HaTzaddik? It is because, unlike their parents and grandparents, Ephraim and Menasheh grew up in *galus*, in an exile that was so contrary to the people and values they represented, yet they merited to become counted as two of the *Shevatim*. We give our children the blessing that in times and places where they find themselves among foreign cultures and ideologies, they remain true to their heritage and their mission in the world. This is true success in this world as we await the time when the entire world will reflect the *emes* we carry with us.

The Antidote

The greatest antidote to withstanding the pressures and shallow attractiveness of the outside culture is living a Torah lifestyle *b'simchah*. Giving over a feeling of *simchah* in general, and specifically in terms of one's Torah observance, is a powerful gift that one can give their children. It is the tool that will allow them to remain firmly committed to a Torah way of life, not only out of a sense of obligation, but because they are motivated to do so; they will *want* to live that way. *Simchah* is a very deep *middah*. We cannot conclude that just because someone is always smiling and cheerful that they are truly *b'simchah*. And our children will always the know the difference between our smiling politely to our friends and neighbors and even to them (and there is nothing wrong with that) and true *simchah* that permeates us as people and affects all the areas of our lives.

Simchah is an inner serenity that reflects the knowledge that we are doing what we should be within the context Hashem has given us. In instilling *simchah*, our goal should not be to have our children always "happy" and having fun at all times. We do not have to be concerned if they are having a rough day, don't like their teacher, or don't want to do the chore we just requested of them. These are all parts of real life and are very beneficial experiences for children to go through with our guidance. If a child doesn't like their teacher, instead of running to switch classes, it may be a good opportunity to teach them how to deal with someone they don't necessarily relate to, especially when that person is an authority figure. If a child complains about doing a chore that we have previously discussed and assigned to them, we don't have to worry that we're being overly demanding and will "break" them by insisting they do it. It will instill responsibility and perseverance and serve them well when this is needed in their lives. We can even share times in our own lives where we faced obstacles and frustrations and were able to navigate through these while maintaining our core sense of well-being.

Given the above, children certainly need to see their parents generally happy, with a positive attitude in life and with regard to mitzvos specifically. Children rely on their parents for a sense of safety, security, and orientation in attitude and mentality toward the world around them and within their own lives. Imagine it is the week before Yom Tov. What is our attitude, tone, and energy like? Are we anticipating the upcoming holiday, looking forward to extra family time, busy with preparations? Or are we short-tempered due to high levels of stress, dreading Yom Tov, and sharing these sentiments with our family. And what about when we are actually in a Yom Tov or a long Shabbos during the summer months? Do we talk about how we long for it to be over, how we can barely wait to get back to our regular weekday schedule? It is normal for the holidays and even Shabbos to be a busy and more hectic time. But what messages are we sending our children about what the experience of Shabbos and Yom Tov should be? We need to ask ourselves—what do we need in order to bring *simchah* into our home for Shabbos and *Yamim Tovim*? When we experience joy and are thankful for these opportunities Hashem has given us to connect more deeply with Him and with those closest to us, we can then begin to try and transmit this to our children. Words about the holiness or specialness of the holidays or of Shabbos will ring hollow unless we are living examples of this reality.

Beyond the Jewish calendar, we can think more broadly about what mitzvos or aspects of Judaism we really relate to or feel inspired by. Articulate what it is you feel especially and naturally connected to.

Even these sentiments can be phrased in age-appropriate terms and it will give your children a language they can emulate and internalize for themselves. Making *simchah* a reality that is felt in the home begins by identifying and then expressing our own feeling of *simchah* in living a Torah life as a member of the special nation of Klal Yisrael. One caveat to keep in mind is that there is no reason to be concerned if our children do not immediately reflect our happiness in Jewish living. If our joy is real and consistent, they will internalize it over time.

Addressing Shortcomings

Even if our home is a haven of warmth and positivity, it is inevitable that our children will come into contact with some of the shortcomings that exist *within* the observant community. It is important to note that we are not addressing instances of abuse of any kind. Abuse in any form must be dealt with as a separate topic with a relevant and appropriate approach. Here we are addressing the idea of shortcomings existing in any communal, educational, social, *shidduch*, or other "system." On one hand, we do not have to, and should not, pretend that any system is perfect. On the other hand, we have to be careful how we speak about these real or perceived imperfections and how we portray these, especially to our younger children. Similar to the danger in critiquing a spouse in front of one's children regardless of the fact that by definition a human being inevitably carries with them flaws and imperfections, it is extremely detrimental to a young child to have these highlighted in an emotionally laden, tense way. In secular life, and in the public-school system in particular, children's personal lives, including their belief systems, are separate from their interactions with teachers and authority figures. While they learn information from them, they do not look to these individuals as role models of ethical behavior or spiritual accomplishment. In contrast, Jewish day schools are by definition a means to impact the lives of their students in a holistic way. We cannot tear down *rebbeim*, educators, and institutionalized policies that our children need to be able to rely on in order to grow and receive guidance from these very same people and constructs. Children need to feel that their environment is inherently positive, safe, and reliable in order for them to develop as stable and secure adults. What we can do is teach our children that only Hashem and Torah are perfect. People, and the systems they set up, even with the best intentions and loftiest goals, can be imperfect and flawed. This is something we all have to deal with throughout life, and navigating our children through this process will be invaluable to them. Even when a child himself observes issues or shortcomings, we should not deny the reality of these, and we should feel comfortable discussing them with him in a way that is not emotionally charged but rather thoughtful. We can teach our children that thinking critically is in itself a value, and that coming up with a conclusion or answer is not always the most important part. The process can be more important than the result.

> A fourteen-year-old boy whose parents sent him to a yeshiva day school frequently heard his mother expressing her frustration at the school's lack in providing high-level secular studies. At fifteen, and quite unmotivated in his classes, this boy would quote his mother in a condescending and sarcastic tone, "Yeah, my mom takes me to the library so at least I can learn something." This mother could have achieved the same end but without tearing down her child's school and, in the process, much of his Jewish experience with it.

There is a difference between offering constructive criticism as a team player and critiquing the opposing team. Which position are we taking as we discuss what we believe to be shortcomings in a school or other community system? Much like spouses who need to work together for the benefit of the child, parents and school systems need to identify as team players, both making efforts with the child's best interest in mind. The mother of the teenage boy above could have taken her son to the library or otherwise supplemented his secular studies but without the emotionally negative messages about the broader environment, where her child needed to feel a sense of respect in order to thrive. If a parent cannot, for whatever reason, take on a stance of being a team player with the school, shul, or other communal system in which they find themselves, it is worthwhile considering whether a change in institution needs to happen for this family to find a place that will be a good, albeit not perfect, fit.

Insist or Let Go?

Another major consideration that parents have to make on a regular basis is which mitzvos or behaviors we will enforce and "make a big deal about," and in which areas we will allow for more flexibility in our kids' adherence. Our considerations here will obviously change with the age and maturity of our children. A four-year-old who resists *bentching* after a meal should be treated differently than a thirteen-year-old who exhibits this behavior. While the former can be dropped without much pressure or concern, the latter should alert parents to possible larger issues or frustrations the child is experiencing that they are not communicating directly. Our considerations will also be impacted by the expectations, standards, and norms in our community. In this area, in particular, it is extremely helpful for *baalei teshuvah* to have one or more families who are examples of what they are striving for as a family, whom they can approach and ask about what is normal behavior and expectations for a child at any given age within that particular community or ideology.

One qualifying factor that can help guide decisions in this area will be the difference between our ideals and halachah. Sometimes, these will be one and the same. However, many times, if we ask ourselves whether the thing we are expecting or hoping for from our children is, bottom line, what Jewish law expects of us, or something that is beyond that, we will find that much of our goals and dreams for our children lie in the latter. There is no inherent problem with this. In fact, it can be very beautiful to send children the message that we want to go above and beyond the basic letter of the law and truly reflect the spirit of halachah; to become the type of people that adherence to halachah is meant to produce. However, if a child shows resistance to a given expectation, it can be very helpful to identify the category of the behavior or expectation under question. It might be better to show flexibility in the short-term on something that parents would prefer but goes beyond halachah, and in the long run gain a child with a positive attitude toward Judaism who shows greater cooperation and even initiative.

> *The parents of an adolescent boy who had actively stopped keeping mitzvos over the course of several years, would invite boys and girls in their community over to their house on Shabbos in order to try and engage their son while he smoked and played music on his iPod in his room. These parents remembered a time when they yelled and screamed and engaged in tug-of-war arguments when this boy wanted to wear colored shirts or listen to Jewish music that had a non-Jewish flavor to it. They thought wistfully that perhaps had they shown some leeway then, they would not have to go to such painful lengths to accommodate their son now, in an effort to instill some spiritual positivity into an almost nonexistent Jewish life.*

Many times, flexibility in parenting is an investment that pays significant dividends in time.

> *Another family had a ten-year-old child who showed great resistance to davening, especially on days off from school when this was not being enforced as part of the structure and expectation of his school day. His parents realized that every Shabbos and other non-school day was fraught with negativity over whether he would daven properly. They were particularly concerned that the only outcome of this issue would be a feeling of bitterness and resentment directed toward the tefillah experience itself. This seemed completely counterproductive and they decided to seek guidance from a trusted rabbi.*
>
> *They were encouraged to set a baseline expectation for some davening during these days but to leave the exact duration and specific prayers said up to the boy. They were relieved and happy to see a noticeable decline in tension between them in this area, but that in addition to this, over time the boy developed a*

positive attitude toward davening and, more broadly, the idea of communicating to Hashem what was on his mind.

Another good rule of thumb is to consider how this particular situation and my response to it will affect this child for the long-term. A three-year-old who resists washing *al netilas yadayim* is unlikely to have this same issue at thirteen years old if he or she is otherwise happily adjusted in their Jewish life. Therefore, responding to this three-year-old can be simple. Their behavior can be ignored. We can offer them to come join the rest of the family as everyone washes their hands, but we do not have to insist or demand compliance. Likely, this child will eventually want to join in on what everyone else is doing because he won't want to be left out. While extra attention and pressure here can create a bigger issue, letting the whole thing go can allow it to resolve itself on its own smoothly. However, even a young child who exhibits chutzpah (disrespectful behavior) toward his parents needs to be addressed in an age-appropriate way immediately. This is something that can certainly manifest five, ten, and twenty years later if not dealt with early on as part of one's upbringing. We have to keep in mind that our responses to our children today shape their perspectives and attitudes years later, even when the specific behaviors we were addressing are no longer relevant.

Determining which mitzvos and behavior parents will insist on and which they will approach with more flexibility should be a conscious decision-making process, and whatever is decided about any particular issue should be enforced with consistency. If you've decided that your child will daven on days they have off from school and have determined this is a reasonable expectation given their age, ability, etc., then they need to know that this is not negotiable, excluding unusual or extreme circumstances where normal expectations of their behavior in general do not apply. However, if this is something you've decided is nice but not necessary at this point in time, then if it happens, certainly give praise, but demanding they do it would be inappropriate. Parents should also be open to reevaluating these decisions if it seems like whatever they have put in place isn't eliciting a positive response or isn't working in the best interest of their child.

The most important thing to keep in mind is that developing a trusting, warm, and positive relationship with our child is our greatest tool in making parenting decisions that are truly in line with what is best for each individual child. The better we know him or her and really understand who they are and their unique needs, the better equipped we will be to speak and act in ways that are relevant, meaningful, and therefore impactful for them. In so many situations and times in their lives, our children will need us to be their greatest advocate. We need to make sure we have developed a relationship with our child, along with a deep-seated confidence in our ability as their parent, that truly positions us for success. We need to invest time and energy in getting to know each of our children well and strengthening our bond with them, instead of being distracted by external, fleeting behaviors.

Furthermore, we have to remember that we have all of childhood to be *mechanech* our children. We do not need to worry if they aren't doing everything we would like or expect of them right away. With our patience, many things will come on their own. Just like some children potty train earlier while others a bit later, they all get it at some point.

Socialization works to our benefit here as well. There are many things that children will do simply because of their academic and social environment, and in these areas we can and should allow ourselves a greater degree of flex room in managing behaviors. A young child not answering amen to a *berachah*, keeping their *kippah* on their head all the time, or sitting quietly in shul are just several examples of things that may not be the best avenues to direct our parenting energy and focus toward.

> One mother noticed that her nine-year-old daughter showed aversion to wearing knee socks during the summer months despite this being the family's preference and a standard expectation in the school and social environment that she was a part of. This mother took the time to think about the issue in general, and her daughter in particular, without responding impulsively or out of fear. She saw that her daughter was not acting in a defiant way out of anger or malice. She simply didn't like wearing the knee socks in the heat. This mother chose to

let this issue go and just monitor its development. By the next summer, her daughter was wearing knee socks along with all the other girls in her school and camp. She was still hot and not so comfortable in them, but somehow she now found it less unbearable in light of what was considered typical behavior in her surroundings.

Judaism should not be a burden. We need to send our children the message that we love what we are doing and our special lifestyle despite the occasional and inevitable challenges. It is well known that the leader of American Jewry in the previous generation, Rabbi Moshe Feinstein, *zt"l*, attended a bar mitzvah celebration, and, after hearing many long and detailed speeches about intricacies of Jewish law and philosophy, he rose to speak and addressed the bar mitzvah boy with one line, "It's good to be a Jew!" Later, he explained that in the early-to-mid-1900s in America, so many Jews exhibited great *mesirus nefesh* (self-sacrifice) to remain loyal to Jewish observance, but their children saw the pain and struggle that Judaism caused their parents and left a life of Torah and mitzvos. They saw it as a difficult burden rather than a glorious gift. Rabbi Feinstein tried to counteract these messages and re-instill the sense of pride and excitement that was desperately needed to create an enduring Jewish experience.

What Really Matters

The fundamental lesson here is that parenting is so much more about who we are and the lives we build—which our children then experience—than any particular parenting technique or even the wisest lessons and answers. Rabbi Yaakov Horowitz[54] quotes Rav Pam as teaching that *chinuch* is fifty percent *tefillah* and fifty percent *shalom bayis*. This does not imply that we do not need to actively parent. Rather, it puts things into perspective and allows us to create the right priorities for ourselves as parents. It also highlights the importance of building a strong and vibrant marriage, as this creates the foundation for a stable,

---

54   Horowitz, *Living and Parenting*, p. 233.

reliable, and warm home that will serve as the bedrock for growth and development for our children. Our relationship with our spouse creates the environment within which our children will come to perceive themselves and their own goals and dreams, and their ability to reach these in their own lives.

Rabbi Horowitz's statement also highlights that especially in the arena of parenting, we need so much *siyata d'Shmaya*. We need Hashem's direct involvement and assistance that is beyond all the "techniques." We need to develop our relationship with Hashem—and this is what our kids will ultimately inherit through osmosis, simply through their experience of living in the home we created for them. If we want our children to live confident and inspired Jewish lives, with a deep connection to Hashem and their personal purpose in the world, then we first have to be and do this ourselves. The people we are and the lives we have built for ourselves will be the loudest unspoken message we send our children. This does not require perfection, but rather requires sincere movement along this path. Our being vocal about needing God in our lives to help us reach our great and lofty dreams will be a message for our children's need for a relationship with Hashem in their own lives. It will also be the conduit for Hashem's Divine assistance to be felt in our lives. Once we realize that so much of our accomplishments, especially in the realm of parenting, are outside our control, we create more opportunities to reach out to Hashem and experience Him in our lives. With this, we also gain a deeper ability to simply love our children unconditionally, regardless of the degree to which they reflect the images we had of their adult versions when we first held them as newborns. This unconditional love will form the unbreakable link to us, and therefore to the entire Jewish people, that we seek to establish at the core of everything we do with and for our children.

Running
a Frum Household

The operating principle in managing a *frum* household is setting ourselves up for technical success so that all the beautiful *hashkafos* and ideals we had about having a *frum* family have space to develop amid the backdrop of real life. We may value the ideal of having a large family but did not grow up in one or see our own mother manage one. We have to be honest with ourselves about what we can handle. A woman who saw her mother have a child every year has different expectations for herself, her life, and what she can realistically give to each child than a woman who grew up as an only child or with one or two siblings. Neither is better, they are just different. We cannot negate the expectations and needs we have for personal well-being that were implanted within us in a deep way long before we were able to become conscious of them. Furthermore, the need for a *rav* who understands us becomes especially important here. We need to discuss *sh'eilos* around family planning with someone who represents Torah and who sees us for the individuals we are, with our own unique circumstances and abilities. We have to be honest with ourselves so we can in turn be honest with our spouses and with *daas Torah*. Comparing ourselves to our friends or neighbors is not only useless but often quite harmful. Our spouses and children need us—not the mother or father next door—to raise them with a content and wholesome attitude. No one else can or will fulfill this role in our place.

Expectations, Round Two

We have to be cognizant of the need to sometimes cut back on expectations of hosting, tidiness, energy for socializing, or even attending a shiur. This is very real and especially true when there is a new baby or a few small children close in age who demand our time and attention. With regard to other areas, we need to permanently change or adjust our expectations altogether. If Shabbos and *Yamim Tovim* are going to be positive experiences for ourselves and our families, we need to figure out systems that work well for us. While focus on making Shabbos a special time is appropriate, it is unnecessary to stress ourselves out trying to making the fanciest meals in our community, or on our block. Reminding ourselves that we are not trying to replicate the eight-course meal that our rebbetzin once served is important. Nor are we recreating the Thanksgiving dinner our mother made (once a year, with months of advance planning). We do this on a weekly basis, and it needs to be something we begin to develop a routine for, doing it in a way that works for us so we can truly enjoy Shabbos and special times throughout the year. Our family's Purim costumes and *mishloach manos* should be as creative and coordinated as will allow for us and our children to positively enjoy the day. Impressed friends will mean very little in the face of children who feel the holiday is more about reputation and social standing than about them and about appreciating the meaning of the day.

Getting the Kids Involved

Getting the kids involved in household activities and chores is good for both parents and children in the long run. It will teach them responsibility, ownership, and make them feel more capable. This needs to start as young as possible, with age-appropriate tasks, in order to develop important habits, which will be much harder to cultivate as they get older. Often, this requires more effort on our end initially, but eventually the children will become more independent and it will actually be easier for us in the long run. Setting the table for Shabbos, cooking or baking a simple but special dish for Shabbos or Yom Tov, packing lunches for siblings, or helping with getting the baby dressed or changed are just some examples of possible ways to give children responsibilities and build life skills within the home and through daily life. This can be particularly powerful if we are able to pinpoint unique abilities, talents, or interests of each particular child and turn these into something practical that is contributive in nature. This will build them up in a deep way, cultivating their own ability to be capable and giving them a sense of their unique potentials in positively impacting the world around them. A creative child can be assigned to bake and decorate Shabbos dessert or make a "camp" to keep her younger siblings occupied on a busy *erev Yom Tov*. An organized child can be in charge of keeping a running grocery list. A child with intellectual strength in a certain subject can be directed to help a younger sibling with their homework. When each child sees that their unique contribution is needed and expected, they become an active and integral part of a larger whole. Running and managing a household will become practically more manageable, and we will be taking advantage of an opportunity to imbue our children with valuable life skills, and even setting them on the path of being other-oriented throughout life.

Capitalizing on Our Strengths

The more organized we can be, the smoother and easier things can run. Shopping lists, meal planning, and daily and weekly to-do lists and schedules will all be helpful aids in managing our busy, full homes and lives. At the same time, flexibility is also an extremely useful trait to cultivate. The unexpected should be expected as part of a busy and hectic life. All people fall somewhere along the continuum of these two personality types. The same person who manages time efficiently and sticks to their daily schedule to the dot may feel clearheaded as he or she moves through the demands of his or her day. That same person will find themselves flustered and frustrated as one of their children wakes up sick one morning, and suddenly their finely tuned plan for a productive day dissipates as they rush to get the other kids ready for school in time to make it for sick walk-in hours at the pediatrician. In these all-too-common moments, we have two choices:

- We can get stuck in the feeling that our day or plans were somehow ruined or sabotaged by unforeseen circumstances.
- We can take a moment to pause and consider what Hashem wants of us that day. What should our priorities be in that moment, not as we see them, but as part of a larger plan that we are meant to play an active role in.

Rabbi Akiva Tatz[55] teaches an exercise in self-awareness called "enclosing the circle." He instructs readers to draw a circle. Inside the circle we are meant to write all our abilities, talents, and strengths—what we are capable of. Outside the circle we write the things we are not. Artistic, outgoing, organized, for example, may be within the circle for one person and outside it for someone else. You, as one person, are unlikely to be the wife and mother that serves a fancy hot dinner each night, keeps the house neat and tidy, plays on the floor and does art projects with your babies and toddlers, hosts and entertains a myriad of guests constantly, enriches your children with a variety of extra studies and activities, all in one. You are also unlikely to be the husband that is both spontaneous and super-structured, sensitive and laid-back, and also extremely career driven. We have to ask ourselves: What are my unique strengths? What is natural for me? Yes, we will have to work on the character traits that we need to function successfully that are less naturally a part of who we are. But we can start with what we already are before becoming overly focused on what we are not. Once we discover what exists in our unique, personal circle, we can incorporate it into our family life for those closest to us to benefit from these strong parts of ourselves. Our spouses and children do not need a perfect husband and father or wife and mother; rather, a happy and content one.

55   Rabbi Akiva Tatz, *The Thinking Jewish Teenager's Guide to Life* (Southfield: Targum Press Ltd, 1999), p. 79.

Self-care

Self-care cannot be underestimated for people on whom others depend for their well-being and development. We can only give that which we have ourselves. What do we need to feel balanced and internally able to manage? Everyone deals with periodic stress, but someone who is running on empty, constantly depleted and stressed, will not be able to successfully give to those who need them most—their spouse and children. Most people cannot create a "wish list" and expect to receive everything they put on it. Still, we can all put things in place to facilitate our own inner calm and feeling of equilibrium: whether it is an extra hour a week for a *shiur*, a workout class, a few extra babysitting hours, or a coffee date with a friend, we all need fuel in our engines. The fuel can be focused and tailored to our personalities, lives, and needs.

Spouses especially need to ensure that they carve out uninterrupted, quality, alone time. On a weekly or monthly basis this can mean date nights or a lunch meeting over coffee. In addition, there should be times, perhaps once or twice a year, when the couple takes a short trip together *without* the children. These do not have to be lengthy, expensive, or extravagant. They can be for one or two nights and not far from their home. Couples need time to truly connect and reconnect to one another outside the context of being parents. Family trips are fun and memorable, but children need parents who continually work to deepen and strengthen their bond. This is one of the greatest investments a couple can provide for their children. Children will miss their parents for the day or two that they are with family or a babysitter but, unknowingly, they will be gaining far more in the long run. Creating time to positively strengthen your marriage is one of the most important types of self-care that spouses must remember to engage in. Self-care is often more about prioritizing it than the specific resources that are available. Once it becomes seen as a vital ingredient in creating the lives and homes we dream of, the logistics can be taken care of in one way or another. All efforts at establishing inner balance and fulfillment will automatically spill over to impact our families in positive, nurturing ways.

Conclusion

O nce we've arrived at a life of Torah and mitzvos, we realize that, in truth, we've really just begun our journey. As we've climbed and scaled the heights of that great mountain of Torah observance, we've undoubtedly learned many lessons and gleaned insights that have served us well. Perhaps most significant among these is the awareness that our successes and achievements in reaching our current state are most certainly the greatest signal of our capacity to continue to ascend ever higher, from one precipice to the next, as we create a vibrant and meaningful Jewish life. At each stage along the way, new vistas are revealed, greater resilience is realized, and our ultimate destination comes into ever-greater focus and clarity. These are the exact tools that we will need to further ourselves along.

As we strive to become the greatest version of ourselves, we will come to realize that we are not alone in our climb. We will begin to notice others around us, some ahead and some behind, but everyone positively impacted by the energy, insistence, and companionship of our own ascent. The Jewish people need our passion, our talents, and the wisdom we have gained. We need to bring our whole selves to the table with confidence and resolve. As the Gemara says, *"B'makom she'baalei teshuvah omdin tzaddikim gemurim einam omdin—*In the place where *baalei teshuvah* stand, a completely righteous person cannot stand."[56] It is precisely the background and journey of the *baal teshuvah* that creates their unique potential, deep within.

---

56   *Shabbos* 34b.

137

About the Author

Jenny Serle has worked in Jewish outreach, first through NCSY and then J-Life YP, for over a decade. Through guiding many along their *teshuvah* process, she began to focus her efforts on the *baal teshuvah* population. She has developed engaging classes that provide tools and confidence to enable continued growth and success. Jenny currently runs multiple weekly *chaburos*; regularly mentors *frum* young women on issues such as personal growth, dating, marriage, parenting, and more; and is also a trained kallah teacher. Jenny lives in Chicago, IL with her husband and children.